Quantitative Applications in the Social Sciences

A SAGE PUBLICATIONS SERIES

Quantitative Applications in the Social Sciences

A SAGE PUBLICATIONS SERIES

Series/Number 07–150

DIFFERENTIAL EQUATIONS
A Modeling Approach

Courtney Brown
Emory University

SAGE Publications
Los Angeles ▪ London ▪ New Delhi ▪ Singapore

For information:

Sage Publications, Inc.
2455 Teller Road
Thousand Oaks, California 91320
E-mail: order@sagepub.com

Sage Publications India Pvt. Ltd.
B 1/I 1 Mohan Cooperative Industrial Area
Mathura Road, New Delhi 110 044
India

Sage Publications Ltd.
1 Oliver's Yard
55 City Road
London EC1Y 1SP
United Kingdom

Sage Publications Asia-Pacific Pte. Ltd.
33 Pekin Street #02-01
Far East Square
Singapore 048763

Printed in the United States of America

Library of Congress Cataloging-in-Publication Data

Brown, Courtney, 1952–
Differential equations: A modeling approach / Courtney Brown.
    p. cm. — (Quantitative applications in the social sciences, a Sage publications series; 7/150)
Includes bibliographical references and index.
ISBN-13: 978-1-4129-4108-2 (pbk.)
    1. Differential equations. 2. Mathematical models. I. Title.
QA371.B84 2007
515.'35—dc22

                                        2006101376

This book is printed on acid-free paper.

07   08   09   10   11   10   9   8   7   6   5   4   3   2   1

Acquisitions Editor:	Lisa Cuevas Shaw
Associate Editor:	Sean Connelly
Production Editor:	Melanie Birdsall
Copy Editor:	QuADS Prepress (P) Ltd.
Typesetter:	C&M Digitals (P) Ltd.
Proofreader:	Kevin Gleason
Indexer:	Sheila Bodell
Cover Designer:	Candice Harman
Marketing Manager:	Stephanie Adams

CONTENTS

SERIES EDITOR'S INTRODUCTION

Although many of the books in our series are about statistical methods, one departure from this norm is reflected in a small number of the titles dealing with mathematical topics. For example, Nos. 108 and 109 by Hagle provide an introduction to basic math for social scientists, and No. 110 by Iversen has calculus as the focus. A more specialized treatment is No. 27, *Dynamic Modeling* by Huckfeldt, Kohfeld, and Likens, where difference equations are presented to the social scientist. Extending our coverage of mathematics, Brown's *Differential Equations: A Modeling Approach* takes us one step farther by treating time as continuous instead of discrete as with difference equations.

There are some fundamental differences between mathematics and statistics, which used to be considered a branch of applied mathematics, in how they apply in the social sciences even though both use mathematical symbols to express variables, parameters, and functions: Statistical models are characteristically stochastic whereas mathematical models are typically deterministic (though stochastic processes can be incorporated in models such as stochastic differential equations); statistical models assist the social scientist in theory testing whereas mathematical models help the researcher do theoretical exploration and theory building; statistical models involve data reduction (i.e., estimating a few parameters from a large number of observations) whereas mathematical models imply knowledge expansion (i.e., predicting an array of behavioral patterns from a few initial conditions).

Differential equations, then, can be applied to build our theories and expand our knowledge; Brown's *Differential Equations* shows us how this can be done.

In spite of its early development in the 17th century by Leibniz and Newton, the application of differential equations in the social sciences has been much later. For example, the Malthusian population growth model can be cast in terms of a single ordinary differential equation, $dp/dt = rp$, where the size of population, p, is an exponential function of time t and the rate of exponential growth is determined by parameter r. The actual application of differential equations in the social sciences, however, occurred after demographer-ecologist Afred Lotka proposed the two-species predator-prey model in 1925, known as the Lotka-Volterra model. Since then the model has been extended to one for multiple species, and to other kinds of demographic applications. Beyond population studies, differential equations have seen success in the 20th century in the classical arms race model by mathematician-physicist-psychologist Lewis Fry Richardson (illustrated in the current book and in discrete form in No. 27 on difference equations) and in the mathematical model of the Durkheimian division of labor in society by sociologist Kenneth Land, among many others such as the analyses of social, cultural, and technological diffusion and the spread of rumors.

Brown's addition to the series thus serves not only to cover a topic we did not use to have a book for but also to challenge the social scientist to step out of the variable-oriented mindset to think more in terms of processes, an understanding of which is no doubt crucial for a proper understanding of humans' political, psychological, and social behavior.

—Tim F. Liao
Series Editor

ACKNOWLEDGMENTS

My interest in differential equations began in the 1970s with the reading of Isaac Asimov's science fiction *Foundation* series. I am grateful to Dr. Asimov for writing his fiction in such a way that it inspired me to investigate how to model real social systems. Richard DeLeon, my first mentor in political science at San Francisco State University, directed me to study such mathematical systems under John Sprague at Washington University in St. Louis. I am grateful to Richard for giving me such good guidance and to John for helping me pursue this interest. I also want to thank Hank Heitowit at the University of Michigan who invited me for 12 years to teach nonlinear dynamical systems at the ICPSR Summer Program. Finally, the series editor, Tim F. Liao, helped shepherd this manuscript with particular care, and the anonymous reviewers gave exceptionally useful advice, for all of which I am deeply grateful.

DIFFERENTIAL EQUATIONS

A Modeling Approach

Courtney Brown
Emory University

1. DYNAMIC MODELS AND SOCIAL CHANGE

Humans live in continuous time. All social phenomena manifest in the context of continuous time. Differential equations model change in continuous time. The widespread use of differential equations to model social and political change can open up vast new vistas of pioneering research in the social sciences. Understanding that such widespread use has not yet occurred is the social science equivalent of hearing from a reliable source that unclaimed gold is available for the taking in a given mountain setting.

Throughout the physical and natural sciences, scientists routinely use differential equations to model change with respect to all sorts of phenomena. They do this not because all the phenomena that they study exhibit processes of change that are dynamically unique and different from social and political processes. For example, contagion and diffusion processes can occur in chemical reactions just as readily as they can manifest in social settings. Rather, physical and natural scientists use differential equations because they want their models to approximate most closely the continuous-time nature of the real-world phenomena that they study. That is, the phenomena themselves dictate the use of differential equations.

Social scientists also study change, and there have been some highly noteworthy instances of social scientists using differential equations to model processes of change. Many of these seminal instances have become permanent fixtures in the extant social science literatures as examples of brilliant theoretical thinking. The arms race model of Lewis Fry Richardson is one such example.

Nonetheless, the extent to which differential equations are used in the social sciences is nowhere near that of the natural and physical sciences. There are two primary reasons for this. One reason is theoretical and the other is legacy. In terms of the former, a great deal of early empirical research in the social sciences has its grounding in the emergence of population surveys that were conducted in the 1950s (e.g., Berelson, Lazarsfeld, & McPhee, 1954; Campbell, Converse, Miller, & Stokes, 1960). Researchers analyzed these survey data using techniques such as cross-tabulation tables and diverse forms of correlational analysis. This early empirical research led to tremendous advances in our understanding of society and social processes. The methodological approaches adopted by this research consequently led to the now dominant application of regression models that appear in much of the extant social science empirical literature. For these theoretical reasons, social scientists have long been trained to use statistical models that do not rely on differential equations, and the focus on statistical training is now a historical legacy of the development of commonly applied social science methodologies. But given the fact that many social and political processes of change occur in the context of continuous time, it is logical to assume that the potential for discovering important new findings within the social sciences will increase dramatically as social scientists more commonly use continuous-time models of change that closely parallel the dynamical structure of the processes under investigation.

One of the primary purposes of this book is to introduce differential equation modeling to a wider audience in the social sciences. Moreover, I write this book with the full expectation that social scientists who increasingly use differential equations in their models of social and political change will open themselves up to new avenues of theoretical thinking, and that these new avenues of thought will lead to a host of important discoveries. It is also worth noting that theory-building graphical techniques originating from systems theory exist that can assist social scientists in developing differential equation models that embrace high levels of theoretical complexity and nuanced sophistication (see especially Brown, 2008; also Cortés, Przeworski, & Sprague, 1974).

It is normal for social scientists to ask what advantages the study of differential equations may have over other approaches to specifying change over time. Two types of equations are normally used to express change in terms of time: differential equations and difference equations. Differential equations are different from difference equations because they specify time in a continuous rather than a discrete manner. Other than that, differential equations and difference equations are more similar than they are dissimilar. Thus, much of this book is conceptually applicable to the study of difference equations as well, although the mechanics of working with difference equations differ from those used with differential equations. Both differential and difference equations also work with independent variables other than time, but since the dominant application of such equations is with respect to time, this book focuses on that use. Before diving into the mathematics of differential equations, it is worth spending some time outlining more specifically why social scientists might want to use differential equations in the first place.

Theoretical Reasons for Using Differential Equations in the Social Sciences

While it is more common for social scientists to work with statistical models than with differential equation models, it would be wrong to claim that one form of modeling is superior to another. Each approach to modeling has its own advantages and disadvantages. Statistical models are tremendously useful in terms of testing empirical theories, especially when attempting to identify causal relationships between variables through the use of some form of correlational analysis. Thus, when we want to know if hours spent reading causes an increase in reading comprehension test scores, a statistical model that correlates the former with the latter is the approach of choice.

But there are also reasons why a social scientist may be inclined to use a statistical model in situations in which a differential equation model might be more appropriate or perhaps simply more interesting. Many statistical models can be applied "out of the box." The ease with which this can be done may inadvertently encourage some social scientists to avoid working with (and thinking about) more interesting and nonlinear deterministic dynamic model specifications, especially continuous-time specifications.

One of the most important reasons for working with differential equation models is theoretical. Social scientists can use differential equations to develop theories of social and political phenomena that are particularly rich with respect to the specification of time-dependent processes. Of course it can be argued that statistical models also address social theory, and indeed they do. But in general, statistical models are more confined in functional form in a manner that is quite alien to differential equation models. There is a practical and important reason for this. Statistical models must be applicable to a wide variety of empirical settings, and thus the analytic solutions to such models need to be known in their entirety in the form of programmable formulae in advance of any empirical testing. This requirement forces most statistical models to adhere to known functional forms for which the probabilistic mathematics are entirely known and mathematically tractable, a topic I address more fully below. But this requirement is usually not applicable to differential equation modeling. Indeed, with differential equations, the specification of a model is limited only by a researcher's creativity with respect to social theory. Due to advances in both mathematical theory and computing technology, it is now possible for a researcher to work with differential equation models that address social and political theories of unprecedented complexity and sophistication.

A growing number of social scientists now use differential equations to model social phenomena, and even a short and partial list of such applications demonstrates the great variety and depth of these efforts. Some of the classic examples of the use of differential equation modeling in the social sciences include the landmark treatments by Simon (1957), Coleman (1964), and Rapoport (1983). In the field of international relations, Richardson's (1960) classic treatment of arms races remains a frequently cited application of differential equation modeling. Also, Przeworski and Soares (1971) explore a variety of specifications using differential equations that address the dynamics of class consciousness and the left vote. From a sociological perspective, Tuma and Hannan (1984) discuss a variety of methodological approaches to the study of social dynamics using differential equation systems. Gottman, Murray, Swanson, Tyson, and Swanson (2003) exploit both differential and difference equations to examine the psychological dynamics of marriage. Kadera (2001) uses differential equations in an award-winning treatment of political interstate rivalries. Brown (1994, 1995a) uses differential equations to model environmental degradation as a consequence of political decisions to either exploit or defend the environment. Brown (1987b, 1988, 1991, 1993, 1995a) also uses differential equations to "re-create" the dynamics of partisan struggle *between* elections when using both survey and aggregate data for situations in both the United States and the Weimar Republic. (This is called a "boundary-value problem.")

More generally, there are many reasons why a researcher might want to develop a model that specifies time in a continuous manner. Social scientists often think in terms of discrete units of time because data involving societies are frequently collected in intervals of substantial lengths. For example, census data are normally collected every 10 years, and electoral data are collected every few years. But many processes of change are continuous in nature, and there are instances in which social scientists need to use differential equations to model this type of social change. This requires that social scientists take into account the fact that measurements of a continuous process may be conducted in discrete intervals merely for matters of convenience. In such situations, using difference equations to model a continuous-time process of change can sometimes significantly alter the specification of time away from its reality, which in turn can result in a loss of understanding of that which is being investigated. (See especially, Brown 1995a, Chap. 2, for a detailed discussion of this.)

An Example

Let us begin our discussion of differential equations with an example that can demonstrate how powerfully even a simple single-equation differential equation model may address a sophisticated theory. There is currently a great deal of concern these days about the subject of global warming. Carbon dioxide and other heat-trapping gases are being released into the atmosphere through human activity. Global warming has the potential to drastically alter the ability of human civilization to continue to develop without encountering highly unpleasant challenges. Indeed, if global warming continues as many scientists are saying it is progressing, we may be facing a situation in which many coastal cities will need to be evacuated due to rising sea levels. Imagine a world in which the only way to travel down 5th Avenue in New York is with a canoe or scuba gear! Where will the capital of the United States be relocated once Washington, D.C. is flooded? If the U.S. capital is relocated to, say, Atlanta (which is safely 1,000 ft above sea level), will Atlantans lose their representation in the U.S. Congress in the manner in which residents of Washington, D.C. currently lack voting representation? What will happen to the global weather with all that water and heat thrown into the mix? And what will happen to our food crops when the weather turns sour? The possible consequences of global warming are as countless as they are bone chilling. These are all interesting questions that serve as motivation to understanding the following example of a differential equation model.

The following model was developed by Anatol Rapoport (1983, pp. 86–91) to study the growth of pollution and its effect on both human population numbers and the quality of life. Rapoport also uses this model to extend similar theoretical and pioneering discussions initiated by Jay W. Forrester (1971). Let us consider heat-trapping gases a form of pollution, and let us label the level of this pollution with the variable P. (Here, I use the original notation offered by Rapoport.) We are interested in modeling change in this variable with respect to time. One approach is to state simply that there will be a constant rate of release of this pollutant into the environment. In this respect, this is a conservative model since the rate of release will actually grow as human industrial activity increases over time. But even with this conservative simplification, Rapoport's model holds surprising consequences. We can describe this constant rate by writing change in the level of heat trapping pollution as

$$dP/dt = I,$$

where I is the constant rate of pollutant released into the atmosphere.

But carbon dioxide does not simply stay in the atmosphere forever. It is eventually absorbed by plants. Thus, we need to incorporate into our model some means of reducing the level of heat-trapping pollution. A straightforward approach is to say that the rate of decrease will be proportional to the level of the pollutant. Thus, plants will absorb more carbon dioxide when there is more carbon dioxide to absorb since an increased concentration of this gas will assist plants in their growth processes. Mathematically, we can write this as

$$dP/dt = I - aP,$$

where a is a constant parameter, and the term $-aP$ reflects the removal of carbon dioxide from the atmosphere because of its being absorbed by plants.

This is a "safe" model with a happy ending, in the sense that it has a tidy equilibrium. That is, change in the growth of pollution will cease when $dP/dt = 0$, which will occur when $I = aP$. Thus, as the pollution levels grow, the rate of decrease (aP) will eventually equal the constant rate of increase (I), and the overall growth of pollution will stop. But is this realistic? Is it not the case that when the level of carbon dioxide builds up in the environment, there will also be consequences that will inhibit the growth of plant life? For example, increases in carbon dioxide will coincide with increased industrial activity that will result in lots of forests being chopped down. Concomitant human activity will also result in other forms of pollution that will harm plant life.

Because of the collateral effects, we probably want to say that the rate of decrease in the levels of carbon dioxide will not simply be proportional to the level of P. Rather, we will want to say that the parameter a is no longer a constant, but rather it assumes a value that decreases as the level of P increases. One way to specify the decreasing effectiveness of the parameter a in reducing the level of carbon dioxide from the atmosphere is to write this parameter as $a = a_0 e^{-kP}$, where a_0 is an initial value for this parameter (i.e., when $P = 0$) and k is a constant parameter. Note that as the value of P grows larger, the value of e^{-kP} moves asymptotically toward zero. Rapoport's pollution model then becomes

$$dP/dt = I - a_0 P e^{-kP}.$$

Initially, the rate of increase (I) for the pollutant will cause P to increase, and the partial term $a_0 P$ will tend gradually to slow this growth as in the case of the previous version of the model. But as P continues to grow, the term e^{-kP} will increase in importance, and the entire term that describes the reduction in carbon dioxide due to absorption by plants ($-a_0 P e^{-kP}$) will approach zero, leaving only the constant rate of growth, I. This allows P to grow unbounded, and this is a formula for planetary disaster. Crucially, we can understand that this consequence from a simple model has a great deal of realism built into it. Fully understanding this model can make one think seriously about global warming in new and profound ways.

Much more can be done in terms of analyzing Rapoport's pollution model. However, it is already clear from even this short discussion that differential equations can capture highly complex and nuanced theoretical ideas. The differential equation model above adds a great deal of theoretical richness to our understanding of some of the dynamic complexities of the problem of global warming. It is hard to imagine doing the same thing with a linear regression model. A linear regression model can be used to address other issues related to global warming, such as finding a correlation between carbon dioxide levels and atmospheric temperature increases, and this too is a crucially important scientific aspect of the overall issue. So we clearly are not minimizing the importance of statistical models when we use differential equations. Indeed, all social scientists I know who use differential equations also work with statistical models. But the idea of using differential equations to contribute uniquely to the process of theory building is a general characteristic of differential equation modeling. One should also note that it is entirely feasible to estimate the parameters of differential equation models (although this is not done in this book), making them fully complementary to statistical models.

The Use of Differential Equations in the Natural and Physical Sciences

While the focus of this book is the application of differential equations in the social sciences, such deterministic models have long been a mainstay of mathematical analyses in the natural and physical sciences, and it is worth making a brief mention of this use here. With respect to the natural sciences, differential equations have been used extensively in population biology to study the interactions of species in model ecosystems (see May, 1974). The well-known predator and prey equations of Lotka (1925) and Volterra (1931) fall into this category. The use of differential equations in biology is algebraically similar in many respects to the application of such equations in epidemiology. Epidemiology is fundamentally concerned with the spread of disease. Infectious diseases can spread through a variety of diffusion and contagion mechanisms which are readily modeled with differential equations. The seasonal and other periodic aspects of disease spread are also well suited to such equations. In physics, differential equations have been used extensively in countless settings going all the way back to Newton. Indeed, Newton's second law stating that force equals the product of mass and acceleration ($F = ma$) is a second-order differential equation (since velocity is a derivative, and acceleration is the derivative of velocity). Most of these differential equation models are deterministic.

Interestingly, natural and physical scientists are currently expanding their use of probabilistic and statistical models that have long been a mainstay of the social sciences, and it is natural to ask if this means that deterministic models are losing some of their usefulness. For example, many of the contemporary needs of physicists from probabilistic and statistical points of view are being driven by new discoveries in quantum mechanics. They have discerned that quantum phenomena are fundamentally probabilistic in nature. This goes back to a famous theorem by John Bell that helped to determine that the Einstein, Podolsky, and Rosen debate with Neils Bohr was truly and finally resolved (see Aczel, 2001). It was only in the 1980s and 1990s that experimental results for the phenomenon known as "entanglement" demonstrated unambiguously that Einstein's belief that the quantum universe is fundamentally deterministic is incorrect, and that there are no hidden local variables that can explain the entanglement phenomenon. Thus, quantum phenomena place an added emphasis on the use of probabilistic and statistical methods. But despite this increased interest in probabilistic models, physicists still use deterministic methods to model quantum and other phenomena. In particular, they continue to exploit the full range of differential equation approaches, both probabilistic and deterministic. One reason physicists seem to be drawn toward the use of more statistics is that they want to include more statistical measures with their differential equation models. They are not limiting their use of differential equations. Thus, in large measure, as social scientists increasingly use differential equations, and as natural and physical scientists expand their use of probabilistic and statistical models, the types of mathematics that are commonly encountered in all the sciences (including the social sciences) are becoming much more similar across disciplines.

Deterministic Versus Probabilistic Differential Equation Models

Why should social scientists use deterministic mathematics? This is a question that has long been debated within social science circles (see Coleman, 1964, pp. 526–528). Quite honestly, most of the debates appear to have been "won" by the advocates of probabilistic mathematics who usually drown out the determinists both quantitatively (by having the greater number of supporters) and argumentatively (by positing the inherently stochastic nature of social phenomena). The latter point might at first seem to clinch the case for the probabilistic side, but the answer to the debate is not nearly so clear cut. The real answer to this always boils down to the issue of specification richness. Remember that all mathematical models, both deterministic and probabilistic, are approximations of more complex processes. It is an essential feature of any model-building enterprise that many factors are ignored in any model so that the most important ingredients may be captured with some degree of parsimony. The bottom line then becomes the degree of complexity that can be captured by each modeling strategy (deterministic vs. probabilistic) such that the finished mathematical model most closely represents the real-world process that it approximates. My basic argument (which I explain further below) is that the relatively greater algebraic richness that is possible with deterministic mathematics more than compensates for any informational loss that is a consequence of dropping the more complex probabilistic baggage that accompanies stochastically oriented models.

With deterministic mathematics, one can specify models that are much more algebraically nuanced than is possible with most stochastic models. Stochastic models are also equations, but the only ones that can effectively be used in most settings are the algebraically tractable statistical variety. This is because stochastic models are built upon a foundation of probability distributions. Incorporating probability distributions directly into a model increases its complexity greatly, with even modest increases in specification richness quickly producing models that are hopelessly intractable. That is, stochastic models are useful only if they are accompanied by algebraic solutions to their parameters that can be programmed into standard statistical software. Such software is typically designed to evaluate correlations between variables, thereby identifying causal ingredients with respect to a dependent variable. The models themselves are generally "plug and chug," in the sense that researchers can put their own variables into predefined positions of an algebraic form. But when one develops a deterministic model, one dives into the realm of algebraic variety to a degree that can rarely be imagined with stochastic models. This often requires an abandonment of the "plug and chug" estimation programs that are so useful with simpler models. (See also Brown, 1991, Chap. 3.)

There is yet another aspect to this debate. While stochastic models are theoretically bound to at least one random variable, their specifications are nonetheless structured around an inner deterministic "core," that is, a deterministic form combined with a stochastic component. In terms of this core, the primary thing that normally marks one model as "deterministic" and another as "statistical" is that the deterministic model usually ends up being more algebraically nuanced than the core components of the statistical model. For example, the equation of a line is deterministic, and equations of lines are the bedrock of most statistical models. The simplicity of the linear form enables statisticians to solve explicitly for the parameters of the equations (e.g., the slopes and intercepts). Statisticians can also associate probabilistic assumptions with such models. The explicit solutions for the parameters, plus the incorporation of probability distributions into the models, together act to transform a deterministic core of the model into a statistical one. But to do all this, one has to work with a model that is amenable to finding explicit solutions for the parameters, and the probability distributions associated with the various parts of the model similarly have to be approachable. One does not have to develop a very complicated model before all of these things are no longer feasible using probabilistic mathematics.

The real reason for wanting to work with deterministic models then resolves to a desire to develop interesting model specifications that correctly explain social phenomena, but for which there may not be a "plug and chug" statistical counterpart. With such models, specific probabilistic assumptions may be impossible to apply, and the probabilistic distributions associated with the model and its parameters may be unknown. But the algebra of such models is the core of their value. The algebra of deterministic models can be as nuanced as necessary in order to capture the essence of the social phenomena being examined. Indeed, any statistician will tell you that the greatest mistake any modeler can make is to misspecify a model in the first place. The parameter estimates of a misspecified model are often worthless. Thus, if a researcher has a nuanced theory that explains a social phenomenon, then that researcher is much better off working with a deterministic model that captures that theory correctly than a statistical model that sloughs off the nuanced aspects of the theory in order to make use of a plug and chug estimation program.

We talk about differential equations as being "deterministic" because only the most elementary of such models have exact statistical counterparts. Fortunately, the field of deterministic mathematics has advanced greatly in recent years, and it is now possible to estimate fully nearly all deterministic models. This includes conducting significance tests on all of the parameter estimates. Thus, the gap between deterministic models and statistical models is shrinking in practical terms, and the day may arrive when one will simply be able to talk about a model as a "model" rather than as a deterministic or a statistical model.

Differential equations come in both deterministic and probabilistic varieties. This book focuses on only deterministic differential equations.

Probabilistic differential equations are different from their deterministic counterparts in basically two respects. First, with probabilistic differential equations, one models the probability of an event occurring. Thus, probabilistic models give birth to whole events. But with deterministic models, one directly models the event itself (not the probability of the event), and it is possible to predict a fraction of an event. This is normally not a problem except in situations in which event counts or population sizes are very small. (See Mesterton-Gibbons, 1989, for a detailed discussion of this.)

Second, probabilistic differential equations offer some descriptive richness that their deterministic counterparts lack. Both, the probabilistic and deterministic versions, offer mean predictions. But only probabilistic models supply formulas for variances to go along with these mean predictions. Again, the trouble is that there exists an enormous increase in algebraic and computational difficulty when using probabilistic differential equations (see Brown 1995b, Chap. 1), and this is true even with the simplest of such models. More complicated probabilistic model specifications quickly become intractable from a mathematical perspective. It is essential to emphasize that the variance associated with mean predictions is all that is lost by using deterministic models. Again, a broad range of statistical measures can still be employed with deterministic models, complete with full capabilities for estimating the values of the parameters together with their statistical significance. Ultimately, modeling phenomena with deterministic differential equations allows us to investigate much more interesting and complex algebraic specifications than would otherwise be possible from a probabilistic perspective. Thus, when using deterministic models, we gain a tremendous amount of specification flexibility while losing only a small amount of probabilistic richness.

What Is a Differential Equation?

With elementary algebra, equations are normally written to specify a dependent variable as a function of one or more independent variables. For example, the equation $y = mx + b$ is the equation of a line in which y is the dependent variable, x is the independent variable, m is the slope of the line, and b is the intercept of the line. However, a differential equation is one in which a derivative also exists in the equation. Thus, Equation 1.1 is a differential equation.

$$dy/dt = ay \qquad [1.1]$$

In this equation, y is the dependent variable, t (time) is the independent variable, and a is a parameter. In this instance, we are not given an equation that defines the value of y, but rather we are given an equation that defines change in y. Thus, Equation 1.1 says that the rate of change in y depends on the value of y itself. As the value of y increases, its rate of change will also increase (as long as the value of the parameter a is positive). This type of equation is called an "ordinary differential equation" since it contains only an ordinary derivative and not a partial derivative. An equation that contains a partial derivative is called a "partial differential equation." A partial derivative might look something like $\partial y/\partial x$. In this book, we examine only ordinary differential equations. In some texts, the abbreviation "ODE" is sometimes used to reference the words "ordinary differential equations." To ease exposition, throughout this book, the words "differential equations" will simply refer to ordinary differential equations.

Note that in Equation 1.1 the independent variable does not appear explicitly on the right-hand side. This type of differential equation is said to be "autonomous." If the independent variable t appears in the equation as an explicit variable, then the equation is "nonautonomous." Equation 1.2 would be a nonautonomous version of Equation 1.1.

$$dy/dt = ay + \cos(t) \qquad [1.2]$$

The ordinary differential equation 1.1 is also called a "first-order" differential equation. The order refers to the order of the highest derivative appearing in the equation. In this instance, the highest derivative is dy/dt. Equation 1.3 is a second-order differential equation since the highest-order derivative in the equation is d^2y/dt^2. In such equations, lower-order derivatives also may or may not be present.

$$d^2y/dt^2 = ay \qquad [1.3]$$

A differential equation can also be referenced by degree. Sometimes a derivative in an equation is raised to a power, and the magnitude of this power is called its "degree." The degree of a differential equation refers to the algebraic degree of the highest-order derivative in the equation. Thus, Equation 1.4 is a first-order differential equation of degree 2.

$$(dy/dt)^2 = ay \qquad [1.4]$$

The notation in Equation 1.4 is a bit awkward. Thus, sometimes various authors will use the form y' to refer to the first derivative, y'' to refer to the second derivative, and so on. Thus, Equation 1.4 might be more economically written as

$$y'^2 = ay. \qquad [1.5]$$

There is yet another way a derivative may be written. Sometimes a derivative is written with "dot" notation, as is often the case when time t is the independent variable. For example, Equation 1.1 could be rewritten using Newton's "dot" notation as

$$\dot{y} = ay.$$

To offer consistency in presentation, only the notations as shown in Equations 1.1 and 1.5 are used in the remainder of this book.

A differential equation is linear if its algebraic form contains only additive combinations of its variables together with appropriate parameters. Everything else is nonlinear. Thus, a linear differential equation cannot contain powers or interactive terms with respect to the independent or dependent variables. Thus, Equations 1.1 and 1.3 are examples of linear autonomous differential equations of degree 1, whereas Equation 1.6 is a nonlinear autonomous first-order differential equation of degree 1. More exactly, one would say that Equations 1.1 and 1.3 are linear in the dependent variable y, whereas Equation 1.6 is nonlinear in y.

$$dy/dt = ay^2 \qquad\qquad [1.6]$$

In this book, we focus our attention on first- and second-order linear and nonlinear differential equations of degree 1. Some of the most profound uses of differential equations can be found in investigations of systems of two or more first-order ordinary differential equations. Indeed, any second-order differential equation can be expressed as a system of first-order differential equations, as I describe in a later chapter. Also, a nonautonomous differential equation can be rewritten as a system of first-order differential equations (again, explained later). Thus, understanding how to work with first-order differential equations (isolated and in systems) is the key to working with many different situations involving differential equations, which is why first-order differential equations are a primary thrust of this book.

Fundamental to the study of differential equations is "solving" the equations. To solve a differential equation traditionally means to find a function that explicitly specifies a rule to determine the values of the dependent variable, not change in the dependent variable. There are methods that can be used to find explicit solutions for a variety of classes of differential equations. It is often useful to know how the solutions for such equations are derived since this allows one to understand many of the general behaviors of differential equation models. For example, Equation 1.1 is a model of exponential growth over time, a process of the sort described by Thomas Malthus (1798) with regard to his concern about population size. Why this equation models "exponential growth" is not immediately clear from an algebraic examination of the differential equation itself. However, this becomes quite evident with an examination of the solution for this problem, as is done in the next chapter.

In terms of first-order differential equations, this book presents the separation of variables technique for finding explicit solutions to some differential equations. Traditionally, texts for differential equations typically spend a great deal of time also explaining a variety of other specialized methods for solving an assortment of differential equation types. But this approach is increasingly falling from fashion. Many (some would say "most") interesting differential equation specifications do not work with any given collection of approaches to determining explicit solutions. In the past, one needed an explicit solution for a differential equation in order to understand its behavior. But current research into differential equations focuses on the behavior of differential equations often for which no explicit solution can be found. This new research has been made possible due to the development of modern computers. Computers are now used to solve differential equations using numerical techniques that do not require explicit solutions for the equations. This book follows this trend by explaining differential equations in terms of their behaviors. Moreover, numerical methods are used throughout this book to solve for these equations, with only two exceptions. The first exception explains the separation of variables technique, and the other explains solutions to systems of first-order linear differential equations. These exceptions are made for heuristic reasons only, and they do not diminish the importance of the numerical methods. Since numerical solutions to differential equations are so important to our current efforts, it is worth spending a bit more time explaining the rationale for their use.

When we model social phenomena using differential equations, we want to extend our modeling efforts well beyond the limits of linear differential equations for which there are straightforward solutions. Equation 1.1 is the simplest of differential equations, and it is not hard to find a solution for it. But it is usually not possible to find a tidy solution (or any solution) for most interesting differential equation problems, and nonlinear differential equations pose special difficulties in this regard. We are fortunate that there are now easily applied computationally based ways to calculate solutions for the dependent variables of differential equation models. Such numerical methods work with nearly all differential equations. One only needs the original differential equation and an initial condition to use these numerical methods.

The number of such numerical methods is quite large and is steadily increasing, with each method having its own particular advantage in computational speed and/or numerical agility. This book covers the three most important of these methods. Indeed, the first two (Euler's method and Heun's method) are used here mostly as heuristic vehicles to help us understand the fourth-order Runge-Kutta method, which is the workhorse of choice in most situations. All of this is explained more thoroughly in the next chapter.

What This Book Is and Is Not

When someone takes a full college course in most subjects, it is normal for the person to remember only a certain proportion of the material from that course, even soon after the course is finished. This book is written to approximate that proportion of knowledge that would be both readily remembered and often used by someone who took a college course in differential equations and then later applied that knowledge in his or her own research. Thus, this book is written to address the core information that one must retain after taking a full course in differential equations to use them in a scientific study. This means that a full course in differential equations and its associated text would cover more information than that which is presented here.

Let me offer an example. In most courses on differential equations, some time would be spent on the existence and uniqueness theorems. That is, when studying a differential equation, mathematicians want to know if the equation actually has a solution, and whether that solution is unique for any given value of the independent variable. This is more important to the theory of differential equations than to their application because proving existence and uniqueness is not too difficult for most reasonable differential equation models. Indeed, it is rare to see an application of differential equations that spends publication space on existence and uniqueness. To include a discussion of existence and uniqueness for the models presented in this book would require that I then omit a significant amount of other information that would be highly valued with respect to the application of differential equations to modeling. Indeed, and for this same reason, it is not uncommon for many books that focus on modeling applications to omit discussions of topics such as existence and uniqueness. While the topics are important, it is assumed that students of differential equations will be introduced to them elsewhere.

A primary focus of this book is on the use of numerical methods to solve differential equation systems, and this focus follows a recent trend among some scholars. While numerical methods are covered in many books on differential equations, the primary emphasis for a traditional approach to differential equations is on deriving methods to obtain analytical solutions to differential equations. Both the more recent emphasis on numerical methods and the traditional focus on analytical solutions are interesting in their own right. But analytical solutions are often difficult or impossible to obtain with all but the simplest of nonlinear models, whereas numerical methods may be applied in any context, linear or nonlinear. For this reason, I offer only a limited treatment of analytical solutions to differential equations.

In particular, this book covers the separation of variables technique in the case of first-order differential equations, as well as the solution to second-order linear differential equations in which there are two real and distinct roots. Solutions of other classes of second-order linear differential equations are also given, but they are not derived. Some mathematicians will disagree with this omission and argue that this treatment is incomplete. However, the derivations of other classes of solutions for the linear case are readily available elsewhere in longer treatments of the subject, and no argument is made here that students of differential equations should limit their exposure to the subject to this one book should they want to extend their studies further. Moreover, some mathematicians have argued that given the fact that the analytical solutions themselves are of little use outside of the linear case, there are heuristic advantages to emphasizing the more universally applicable numerical approaches in a treatment that focuses on modeling applications (see especially Koçak, 1989). Indeed, Blanchard, Devaney, and Hall (2006) have argued that "the traditional emphasis on specialized tricks and techniques for solving differential equations is no longer appropriate given the technology that is readily available," and "many of the most important differential equations are nonlinear, and numerical and qualitative techniques are more effective than analytic techniques in this setting" (p. vii). Let readers be aware at the outset that this book aligns itself with this latter view.

This book also does not cover the broad topic of how to test differential equations with respect to empirical data. Parameter estimation with differential equation models can be quite challenging when compared to the ease with which linear regression models are evaluated. The challenges reside not only with the issue of dealing with continuous time, but also the nonlinear algebraic complexity that so often accompanies differential equation models. Methods of parameter estimation often employ computationally intensive numerical techniques that are quite common in the fields of engineering. Given the modern reality of fast computers, such methods of model evaluation are entirely feasible and more commonly encountered. Useful examples of fully estimated continuous-time differential equation systems together with explanations of the methods used (as well as additional references) can be found in Brown (1995a). (For an accessible yet more general treatment of the subject of model evaluation using numerical methods, see Hamming, 1971. See also Hamming, 1973.)

Despite these limitations, this book is more than simply a primer in the subject of differential equations. Here, I cover the essential material that will likely be considered the most valuable by those who apply differential equations in their own social scientific projects. In essence, if one conducts social scientific research by applying the methods discussed here, it is likely that all (or at least most) of the requisite bases will have been covered, plus some. Thus, while this is not a definitive and complete treatment of ordinary differential equations, it nonetheless is a sufficiently complete treatment such that many practitioners of these methods will be able to satisfy the bulk of their needs with the information contained here. Researchers can then extend their knowledge of this material by using additional sources as required by their own applications.

2. FIRST-ORDER DIFFERENTIAL EQUATIONS

The study of differential equations begins with the subject of how to solve them. There is a reason why we need to solve differential equations, and why we cannot just leave the equations "as is." Since this book approaches the application of differential equations with respect to time, we can say that a solution to a differential equation must be a function of time. Let us say that we have a differential equation dy/dt, then our solution for this equation is the function $f(t)$. This means that we can replace the dependent variable y with $f(t)$. We are interested in the solution for this differential equation because we would like to know a function that will give us the value of the variable y for any given point in time. Our role as scientists requires us to study the values of our dependent variable y, not just change in y. So if we are to study y itself, then we need to find a way to obtain values of this variable.

There are two ways to solve differential equations. The first involves analytical solutions that use indefinite integration, whereas the second involves computationally intensive numerical methods that approach the problem using easily applied techniques of definite integration. We begin the subject of finding solutions to differential equations by exploring analytical solutions to these equations.

Analytical Solutions to Linear
First-Order Differential Equations

Let us begin with an example. Consider the following differential equation:

$$dy/dt = -3y,$$

or equivalently,

$$dy/dt + 3y = 0. \qquad [2.1]$$

Equation 2.1 is a very typical way of writing differential equations, with both the derivatives of y and y on the same side of the equation. One solution for Equation 2.1 is the function $f(t) = 4e^{-3t}$. To demonstrate that this is a solution for Equation 2.1, we need to show that $f'(t) = dy/dt$. Note that $f'(t) = (4e^{-3t})' = -12e^{-3t}$. Now let us rewrite Equation 2.1 by substituting $f'(t)$ for dy/dt, and $4e^{-3t}$ for y, giving us

$$-12e^{-3t} + 3(4e^{-3t}) = -12e^{-3t} + 12e^{-3t} = 0.$$

From this we can see that a solution for the differential Equation 2.1 is $y = 4e^{-3t}$.

Interestingly, $y = 4e^{-3t}$ is not the only solution for Equation 2.1. Readers are encouraged to try the functions $y = 5e^{-3t}$, $y = 6e^{-3t}$, $y = 7e^{-3t}$, or even $y = 1298e^{-3t}$ as solutions for Equation 2.1. You will find that they all work. If we want to find a particular solution for Equation 2.1, then we need one more piece of information. We need to know an initial condition (or initial value) of the dependent variable y. Once we are given the differential equation and its initial condition (normally when $t = 0$), the problem of determining a unique solution to this is called an "initial-value problem."

It is worthwhile noting at this point that a solution for a differential equation is different from the solution for a typical algebraic equation in two crucial respects. First, algebraic equations have solutions that are numbers, whereas the solutions for differential equations are functions. For example, the algebraic equation $3x - 6 = 0$ has the solution that is the number 2. Second, differential equations can potentially have an infinite number of solutions, any particular one of which will depend on an initial value for the differential equation.

Solving First-Order Differential
Equations Using Separation of Variables

If a differential equation is "separable," then an explicit analytical solution can be derived for it using a method called the "separation of variables."

A differential equation is called "separable" if it can be expressed as the product (or quotient) of two functions, each of which depends on only one variable. For example, Equation 2.2 is separable because $g(t)$ depends only on the independent variable t, and $h(y)$ depends only on the dependent variable y. As we will see below, it is also perfectly fine if either $g(t)$ or $h(y)$ does not even appear in the equation.

$$dy/dt = g(t)/h(y) \qquad [2.2]$$

The solution for Equation 2.2 is obtained by rewriting it as $h(y)dy = g(t)dt$ and then integrating this equation as in Equation 2.3.

$$\int h(y)dy = \int g(t)dt \qquad [2.3]$$

It may not at first be clear why we can simply rearrange the differentials in Equation 2.2 so that we can integrate Equation 2.3. Let the functions G and H be the antiderivatives of functions g and h, respectively. That is, g is the derivative of G and h is the derivative of H. Using the chain rule of differentiation, we can then write the derivative of $H(y) - G(t)$ with respect to t as

$$H'(y)dy/dt - G'(t) = h(y)dy/dt - g(t).$$

But note from a rearrangement of Equation 2.2 that $h(y)dy/dt - g(t) = 0$. This means that the derivative of $H(y) - G(t)$ with respect to t also equals zero. Only the derivatives of constants are equal to zero, however. This means that $H(y) - G(t)$ equals a constant, which we can now call C. Since $H(y) - G(t) = C$, we can rearrange this as $H(y) = G(t) + C$. This last statement is exactly the same as

$$\int h(y)dy = \int g(t)dt + C,$$

which is what we needed to prove to show why the separation of variables method works.

The separation of variables method is best introduced with examples, and four different specifications of differential equations for which explicit analytical solutions can be easily derived are introduced below. These specifications are basic components in many commonly encountered advanced differential equation models, and readers are encouraged to study each of these four specifications thoroughly. Indeed, James Coleman (1964, pp. 41–46) has identified these classic specifications as "ideal types" that are widely applicable to the entire class of diffusion models.

Exponential Growth

The first of these four example specifications we have already seen, and it is the specification for exponential growth, $dy/dt = ay$, which is Equation 1.1 in the previous chapter. In this autonomous equation, the variable t does not appear on the right-hand side. But Equation 2.2 still applies because we note that $t^0 = 1$, and thus $g(t) = 1$ in Equation 2.2.

Equation 1.1 has the explicit solution that can be found using traditional methods of integration, as is done below. After separating the variables for Equation 1.1, we have

$$(1/y)dy = adt.$$

This results in the simplified integration problem,

$$\int (1/y)dy = \int adt.$$

The intermediate steps leading to a solution for this problem are

$$\ln|y| = at + C,$$

where C is a constant of integration

$$e^{\ln|y|} = e^{(at+C)} = e^{at}e^C,$$

$$y = \pm e^C e^{at}.$$

At $t = 0$, we have $y_0 = \pm e^C$, where y_0 is the initial condition for the dependent variable. Thus, our solution for Equation 1.1 can be expressed as Equation 2.4. This is called the "general solution" of our differential equation.

$$y = y_0 e^{at} \qquad\qquad [2.4]$$

We are normally given the initial condition for a dependent variable when we are given its differential equation. As mentioned previously, the combination of the differential equation and the initial condition of the dependent variable is called an "initial-value problem." Once you have a solution such as Equation 2.4 and an initial value for y, you can then solve for the "particular solution" of the differential equation. This particular solution gives you a function that allows you to find any value of the dependent variable at any point in time.

For example, let us say that our differential equation is $dy/dt = 3y$. Moreover, let us say that the variable y has the value of 0.1 at $t = 0$. Now we have an initial-value problem since we are given a differential equation

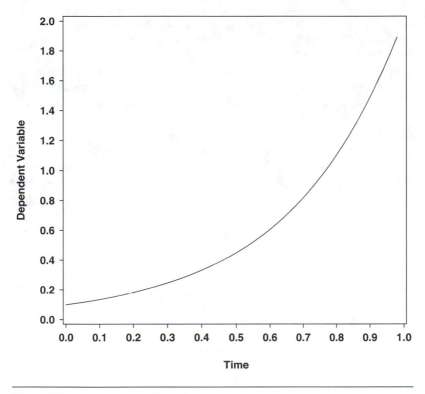

Figure 2.1   Exponential Growth

and its initial condition. We first find the general solution of the differential equation, which is

$$y = y_0 e^{3t}. \qquad [2.5]$$

Since we are told that $y = 0.1$ at $t = 0$, we can substitute this information into Equation 2.5 to obtain the intermediate step, $0.1 = y_0 e^0$, which gives us $0.1 = y_0$. Thus, our particular solution for the differential equation is $y = 0.1e^{3t}$, and we are done. It is now easy to see from this particular solution why the differential equation as given in Equation 1.1 is used to model exponential growth, since the value of y will increase exponentially as time goes from zero to infinity. A plot of this differential equation over time (with $a = 3$) is given in Figure 2.1. This type of plot is called a "time series" because the values of the dependent variable are represented on one of the axes while time is represented on the other axis. The norm is to use the horizontal axis for time, although this is not required. The values for the dependent variable as shown in a time series plot can be found directly from the particular solution of the differential equation by simply supplying various values of the independent variable t.

From Figure 2.1 it is clear that the rate of growth (dy/dt) for the variable y increases over time (and as the value of y increases). This means that the second derivative of y is positive. Potentially explosive properties can result from such processes if left unchecked, and this was the concern of Thomas Malthus with regard to population growth. Situations in which the rate of growth is proportional to the level of the dependent variable are said to be experiencing "positive feedback" (Crosby, 1987). This is because increases in the levels of the dependent variable feed back into the system to produce additional growth in that variable that increases the previous rate of growth.

Exponential Decay

Exponential decay is similar to exponential growth. The only difference algebraically is that the parameter a in Equation 1.1 assumes a negative value. This type of dynamic process can be very important in modeling phenomena in which the rate of decay for a quantity is proportional to the size of the same quantity. Radioactive half-life is a classic example of such a process, but there are many social phenomena which also exhibit decay properties. Indeed, among theorists who study social systems (e.g., Brown, 2008; Cortés et al., 1974), the idea of "system memory" is closely connected to the half-life concept. Systems are typically dynamic in nature, and they respond to various inputs to produce outputs. When an input enters a system, it is natural to ask how long its impact remains in the system, and this is another way of wanting to evaluate the half-life of the system. Essentially, when most events happen, the effect of such events on the relevant social system eventually fades away. For example, riots flare up and then diminish gradually, scandals create a big media sensation but eventually fade from public awareness, many diseases (such as a flu) cause mass illness but then gradually pass out of the populace. More specifically, Przeworski (1975) examines system memory with respect to electoral instability, and Brown (1991, Chap. 7) investigates system memory with respect to the U.S. congressional mobilization cycle. It is useful to note that system memory is equally appropriate for both differential and difference equations.

A time series plot demonstrating exponential decay can be found in Figure 2.2. In this figure, the parameter a in Equation 1.1 is given the value of -3. The initial value for this plot is $y_0 = 1.8$. The half-life of this plot is the time when half of the initial value is gone, the time when $y = 0.9$.

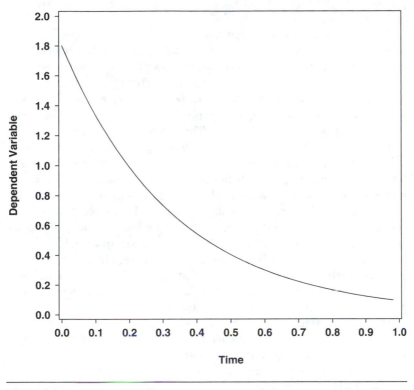

Figure 2.2   Exponential Decay

Learning Curves and Noninteractive Diffusion

When someone is given a new task to do, the person may initially perform the task with a low level of efficiency. For example, the person may run into many unexpected situations that require the assistance of an instructor or supervisor. But as the person continues to work at the task, the person becomes more proficient at it. Initially, training is highly beneficial to this person. But as the person becomes more familiar with the parameters of the task, additional training produces less and less benefit. Thus, the person gradually approaches peak efficiency at doing this task. This process is often modeled with something called a "learning curve" because psychologists use functions that model such dynamics to describe the relationship between experience or training and performance efficiency. The more experience or training someone has in doing a task, the more efficient the person is at performing it. The level of efficiency tends to approach an upper bound over time.

Consider another example that has a similar dynamic process. When a major event is first reported in the news, many people in the populace will learn about the event because there are many people who do not know about it. As time moves forward, steadily fewer new people learn about the event because there are fewer who do not yet know about it. Thus, the rate at which the news of the major event spreads is proportional to the number of people who do not yet know about the event. This is also a learning process, one in which learning is measured in terms of how many people in the populace are being introduced to information about the event. Eventually, fewer and fewer new people will learn about the event even if the news media continues to broadcast the same story. We can say that the number of people who know about the event is approaching an upper bound over time, and the continued broadcast of information about the event will have a steadily decreasing effect on the numbers of new people who learn about it.

Processes of this sort are often modeled with differential equations of the sort shown here as Equation 2.6. Sometimes diffusion models lacking interactive components are specified in this manner as well (see Coleman, 1964, p. 43). (A diffusion model that does contain an interactive component is the logistic model, which I discuss in the next section.) In the learning model, the dependent variable, y, represents the numbers (or proportion) of people who have a certain characteristic, such as the number of people who know about a particular news story. The upper bound of the growth process is represented by U. The quantity $(U - y)$ represents the number of people who do not yet have the characteristic of interest. Finally, the parameter a represents the rate at which people who do not yet have the characteristic of interest become people who do have this characteristic.

$$dy/dt = a(U - y) \qquad [2.6]$$

We can separate our variables for Equation 2.6 by writing the equation as

$$[1/(U - y)]dy = adt.$$

We then integrate this as

$$\int [1/(U - y)dy] = \int adt,$$

yielding

$$-\ln|U - y| = at + C,$$

where C is a constant of integration.

Note that $U - y$ can never be negative since y cannot exceed its upper bound. This is not a mathematical result but a consequence of the context of our substantive problem. Thus, we can drop the absolute value sign and write the equation as

$$-\ln(U - y) = at + C,$$

or equivalently

$$\ln(U - y) = -at - C.$$

This then yields

$$U - y = e^{-at}e^{-C},$$

or after rearranging,

$$y = U - e^{-C}e^{-at}.$$

Since e^{-C} is a constant, we can write the general solution of the model in finished form as Equation 2.7.

$$y = U - Be^{-at} \qquad [2.7]$$

Equation 2.7 is the functional form of a learning curve. Note that when $t = 0, y_0 = U - B$. As time moves forward (i.e., t gets larger), Be^{-at} shrinks to zero in the limit and y approaches U.

A time series plot of this process is shown in Figure 2.3. In this plot, $a = 3$, $U = 1.6$, and $y_0 = 0.1$. Note how the value of the dependent variable, y, approaches the value of U as time moves forward. We can say that y asymptotically approaches the constant value of U over time, which means that y continues to approach its limit, U, with steadily smaller increments without actually ever reaching this limit. This limit is also called an "equilibrium value" of y, since it is a value at which change in y ceases. That is, at $y = U$, then $dy/dt = 0$, as can be seen from an examination of Equation 2.6.

From Figure 2.3 it is clear that the rate of growth (dy/dt) for the variable y decreases over time (and as the value of y increases). This means that the second derivative of y is negative. Such situations are said to be experiencing "negative feedback" (Crosby, 1987). This is because increases in the level of the dependent variable result in diminished rates of growth for that variable. The dependent variable is still growing (since dy/dt is positive), but it grows at a steadily slower rate.

Logistic Curve

The logistic curve is one of the most useful (and heavily exploited) modeling strategies used in the social sciences. It combines exponential growth and decay with the asymptotic approach to a limit that is found in the

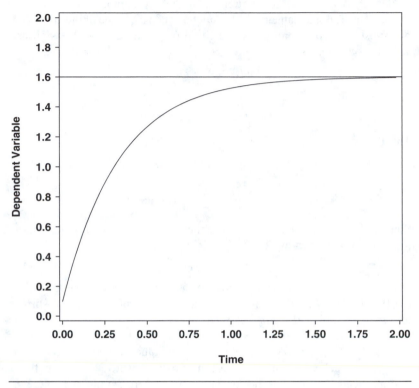

Figure 2.3   A Learning Curve

learning curve. Logistic processes begin with rapid growth characteristic of positive feedback systems, followed by slower growth that is dominated by negative feedback.

The logistic model can be written in a variety of ways. One common approach is to specify it as in Equation 2.8.

$$dy/dt = ay(U - y) \qquad [2.8]$$

In Equation 2.8, U serves the same purpose as it did in the learning curve model found in Equation 2.6. It is the upper bound for growth in y. When the level of y is low relative to U, then the quantity $U - y$ is large, and the rate of growth is exponential. Positive feedback dominates the process during that time. But when the level of y approaches its limit, U, then the quantity $U - y$ approaches zero and the negative feedback dominates.

Social processes that can be usefully described using a logistic model often involve the interaction between people who have one quality with people who do not have that quality. For example, Przeworski and Soares (1971) use a logistic model to describe the interaction of workers who support leftist parties with workers who do not yet support leftist parties. Also, scientists who model infectious diseases often utilize logistic models to describe the process of contagion, where people who have a disease interact with those who do not yet have it. But logistic processes can be found in other settings as well. For example, Brown (1995a, Chap. 6; also 1994) uses a logistic structure to describe processes that lead to the destruction of the environment.

Equation 2.8 is separable, and we can write the integration problem as

$$\int \frac{1}{y(U-y)}\,dy = \int a\,dt. \qquad [2.9]$$

To solve Equation 2.9, it is useful to rewrite the integrand on the left-hand side as

$$\frac{1}{y(U-y)} = \frac{1}{U}\left(\frac{U}{y(U-y)}\right) = \frac{1}{U}\left(\frac{U-y+y}{y(U-y)}\right)$$
$$= \frac{1}{U}\left(\frac{U-y}{y(U-y)} + \frac{y}{y(U-y)}\right) = \frac{1}{U}\left(\frac{1}{y} + \frac{1}{(U-y)}\right).$$

Thus, we can now solve this integration easily by writing

$$\int \frac{1}{U}\left(\frac{1}{y} + \frac{1}{(U-y)}\right)dy = \frac{1}{U}\int \frac{1}{y}\,dy + \frac{1}{U}\int \frac{1}{(U-y)}\,dy = \int a\,dt.$$

Now we have

$$\frac{1}{U}\ln|y| - \frac{1}{U}\ln|U-y| = at + C,$$

which in turn can be rewritten as

$$\frac{1}{U}\ln\left|\frac{y}{U-y}\right| = \frac{1}{U}\ln\frac{y}{U-y} = at + C. \qquad [2.10]$$

We can eliminate the absolute values signs in Equation 2.10 since we know that $U > y$, and y is positive. Multiplying both sides of Equation 2.10 by U and then taking the exponent of both sides gives us

$$\frac{y}{U-y} = e^{Uat+UC} = e^{Uat}e^{UC} = Me^{Uat},$$

where $M = e^{UC}$ is a constant.

Rearranging this to isolate our dependent variable, y, gives us

$$y = \frac{MUe^{Uat}}{1 + Me^{Uat}} = \frac{U}{(1/M)e^{-Uat} + 1}. \qquad [2.11]$$

Since $1/M$ is a constant, we can write $K = 1/M$, and then restate Equation 2.11 as

$$y = \frac{U}{1 + Ke^{-Uat}}. \qquad [2.12]$$

Equation 2.12 is our final form for the general solution for the logistic model.

It is clear that it was more difficult to obtain the general solution for the logistic curve than the general solutions for either the exponential growth or learning curve models. This is the way it is with differential equations. As the models get more complicated, the challenge of finding an analytic solution to the models becomes more serious. Quite soon the challenge becomes impossible to overcome. It is for this reason that it is normal practice to use the numerical methods presented later in this chapter to solve differential equation models.

A time series plot of the logistic model (Equation 2.8) is presented in Figure 2.4. The data for this plot can be calculated using Equation 2.12 or by using the numerical methods presented later in this chapter. In Figure 2.4, the parameters are the same as with Figure 2.3: $a = 3$, $U = 1.6$, and $y_0 = 0.1$.

Comparing Figures 2.3 and 2.4 makes it clear that the logistic model produces a slower initial level of growth that more clearly resembles that of exponential growth. The time series for both the learning curve and the logistic model asymptotically approach the limit, U, which is also an equilibrium point for both models. But the logistic model has a more complex dynamic structure. When the time series for the logistic model begins, positive feedback dominates and the second derivative of the model is positive, which means that the first derivative (i.e., the model itself, Equation 2.8) is increasing over time (also, as y increases). But the second derivative soon becomes negative, which means that negative feedback dominates and the first derivative is decreasing in value over time. The closer the values of y are to the limit, U, the more closely the first derivative is to zero. The point in the curve in Figure 2.4 where the second derivative equals zero is called an "inflection point," and this point defines the boundary between the realms of positive and negative feedback for the model.

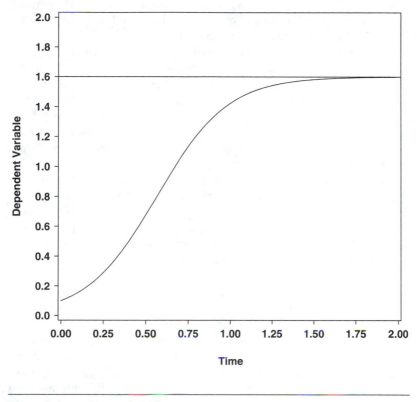

Figure 2.4   The Logistic Curve

An Example From Sociology

Coleman, Katz, and Menzel's (1957) now classic study of the introduction of a new drug into a community of prescribing doctors is a useful example of many of the features of the first-order differential equations described in this chapter. (See also Coleman, 1964, pp. 43–46.) In their study, they are interested in explaining when a doctor will introduce a new drug to his or her patients. A key variable in this respect is whether or not the doctor is integrated into his or her community of doctors. Integration is measured by determining from a sample of the community of doctors how many times a doctor's name is referenced as a friend or as a colleague with whom other doctors interact. Doctors who score high on this measure are identified as "integrated," and doctors who score low on this are labeled as "isolated." Crucially, integrated doctors introduce new drugs to their patients on the average of 4 months earlier than isolated doctors.

Two hypotheses are used to explain this phenomenon. The first hypothesis is that the integrated doctors are more professionally competent, in the sense that they are more up-to-date. So the factors that lead to their integration (professional competence and peer respect) are the same as those that lead to their incorporation of new drugs. The second hypothesis is that the integrated doctors are more able to learn of these new drugs because of their integration. They more often engage in conversations with their colleagues and thus are able to hear about the use of the new drugs more quickly from their colleagues. The isolated doctors need to wait until a drug salesperson knocks on the door and explains about a new drug in persuasive terms.

To test these hypotheses, two models are used. The first is the logistic model, such as given in Equation 2.8. The second is the learning (or noninteractive diffusion) model, such as given in Equation 2.6. When these models are compared with empirical data where one is trying to predict the time it takes for doctors to begin prescribing a new drug, the logistic model describes well the behavior of the integrated doctors, whereas the learning model describes well the behavior of the isolated doctors. For this reason, the first hypothesis is rejected and the second hypothesis is accepted. The integrated doctors adopt new drugs more quickly than the isolated doctors not because the integrated doctors are more professionally competent, but because they interact with their peers more often, thereby receiving information about the new drugs through the process of interactive informational diffusion. Again, the presence of interaction between the exposed and not yet exposed communities is the primary advantage that the logistic model has over the learning model with respect to integrated doctors in this example. The learning model performs better with the isolated doctors because peer interaction is not a factor with these doctors in terms of when they begin prescribing a new drug.

Numerical Methods Used to Solve
Differential Equations

Numerical methods for solving differential equations have been around for a long while. But their use has benefited tremendously from the availability of fast computers. There have also been great advances in the development of new numerical methods in recent years, many of which are more efficient than the older methods. Runge-Kutta methods have long been a primary workhorse for finding numerical solutions for differential equations. Despite their age, they remain exceptionally useful, and they are the starting point for anyone interested in using numerical methods to solve differential equations.

This section presents three Runge-Kutta methods: (1) Euler's method, (2) Heun's method, and (3) a fourth-order Runge-Kutta method. Euler's method is actually a first-order Runge-Kutta method, and Heun's method is a second-order Runge-Kutta. Euler's and Heun's methods are rarely used in practice since a fourth-order Runge-Kutta is both more accurate and easy to use. But understanding Euler's and Heun's methods helps explain how Runge-Kuttas work in general, and they are introduced here heuristically in this regard.

Many social scientists will probably find that a fourth-order Runge-Kutta is a perfect solution to most or all of their differential equation needs, in the sense that such scientists will probably not need to use one of the more modern approaches to finding numerical solutions to differential equations. But, of course, some scientists will undoubtedly still find these more modern approaches interesting, and perhaps preferable, for their own needs. A good starting point for experimenting with these other methods is with a computer program named "Phaser" written by Hüseyin Koçak (www. phaser.com). But the point to be made here from a practical point of view is that many scientists will need to go no further than to understand how to use a fourth-order Runge-Kutta to solve their differential equations. (General discussion of the importance of the Runge-Kutta methods can be found in many treatments of differential equations, but see especially Blanchard et al., 2006; Boyce & DiPrima, 1977, Chap. 8; Koçak, 1989.)

Euler's Method

As with all Runge-Kutta methods of numerical integration, there is no need to obtain an analytical solution to the differential equation when obtaining values of the dependent variable. Runge-Kutta methods can work just as easily with systems of differential equations in which there are a variety of variables that interact with one another. The Euler method is the simplest of all the Runge-Kutta methods, and it is easily explained.

On an intuitive level, the basic idea is that the differential equations (e.g., Equations 1.1, 2.6, or 2.8) are themselves derivatives of dependent variables with respect to time. As derivatives, they are telling us that the values of the dependent variables are increasing or decreasing once we supply whatever is needed for the right-hand side of those equations (such as parameter values). Euler's method works by simply adding a small amount to a current value of the dependent variable to find the next value of this same variable *when the derivative is positive*. On the other hand, when the derivative is negative, we know that the values of the dependent variable must go down, so Euler's method subtracts a small amount from the current value of the dependent variable to find the next value of this variable. Thus, the rule is simple. When the derivative is positive, increase *y*; when the derivative is negative, decrease *y*.

The mechanics of how to do this are not much more complicated than the rule. We are looking for a way to determine the point (t_{next}, y_{next}) from the point (t, y). First, we need a way to move along the time axis to get from t to t_{next}. To do this, we pick a very small number that we will use to "crawl" along the dimension of time. A typically small number to use with Euler's method is 0.01, and greater accuracy can be obtained if this is reduced further. We shall see that this number can be increased significantly for the other Runge-Kutta methods. We use an especially small number for Euler's method because this method is less accurate than the other methods, requiring us to move in very small steps. This small number is called the "step size," and one can think of this number as the size of the steps that we use as we slowly move in time. Thus, to get from time period 0 to time period 1, we need to take 100 steps, with each step being only 0.01 large. The formula for this is $t_{next} = t + \Delta t$, where Δt is the step size.

Now we need to calculate. At each step along the time axis, we want to calculate a value for our dependent variable, *y*. We do this by calculating the next value of *y* given the current value of *y*. Beginning with an initial condition for *y*, we find the next value of *y* based on the direction that the derivative is telling us to go (i.e., up or down in *y*). At this point, we take another step along the time axis and get another value of *y*, and so on. We repeat this process until we have a time series that is sufficiently long to satisfy our needs. This obviously needs to be done with a computer program that contains "loops," which is a way of repeating the same procedure over and over again. With each trip through the loop, we calculate a new value of *y*, save that value for future use, and then repeat the loop again to obtain another new value of *y*, over and over again.

The exact formula for Euler's method is shown here as Equation 2.13.

$$y_{next} = y + h(dy/dt) \qquad [2.13]$$

Equation 2.13 is contained within the computer program's loop that calculates the values of the dependent variable, *y*. In Equation 2.13, the value of *y* on the right-hand side is the current value of this variable given any single pass through the loop. The value of y_{next} is the next value of *y* that will become the current value of *y* in the next pass through the loop. The parameter *h* is the step size. Here we are multiplying the step size by the derivative (which is the original model, such as Equation 1.1), and then adding this to the current value of y to obtain the next value of y. After we calculate the next value of y, we need to remember to save both the current and next values of y, and then to reassign the next value of y to be the current value of y so that the loop can be repeated. We also need to save our current value of time, which is the previous value of time plus the step size, h. Sample computer code (written in SAS, but self-explanatory and adaptable to any language) that does this could resemble the following:

```
DATA;
A=0.3; * The parameter value;
H=0.01; * The step size;
Y=0.01; * The initial condition for the dependent variable, Y;
TIME=0; * The initial value for time;
DO LOOP=1 TO 2000; * The beginning of the loop;
DERIV=A*Y; * The differential equation model;
YNEXT=Y + (H*DERIV); * Euler's method;
TIME=TIME+H; * Incrementing time;
OUTPUT; * Outputs the data in the loop so they can be plotted;
Y=YNEXT; * Shuffles the value of Y obtained by Euler's method
   back to Y;
END; * This ends the loop;
SYMBOL1 COLOR=BLACK V=NONE F=CENTB I=JOIN
PROC GPLOT;
   PLOT YNEXT*TIME;
TITLE "Time Series Using Euler's Method";
RUN;
QUIT;
```

There is a geometric interpretation to Euler's method that is based on the definition of the slope of the line that is tangent to the curve of the model at any given point in time. The model itself is a derivative, and the value of this derivative is the slope of the tangent line. From the definition of the slope of a line, we can say that

$$\frac{y_{next} - y}{t_{next} - t} = \frac{y_{next} - y}{\Delta t} = f(t, y), \qquad [2.14]$$

where $f(t, y)$ is simply our differential equation model. If we rearrange Equation 2.14, we have

$$y_{next} = y + f(t, y)\Delta t,$$

which is the formula for Euler's method as given in Equation 2.13. Some readers may note that Euler's method is also equivalent to the first two terms of a Taylor series approximation for the original differential equation model (see Blanchard et al., 2006, p. 641; also see Atkinson, 1985, pp. 310–323).

At this point it should be clear why Euler's method produces inaccuracies. With each step, Euler's method follows not the curve of the model but the line that is tangent to the curve at a particular point on the curve. The larger the step size, the greater potential there is for Euler's method to move away from the true curve (depending on how "curvy" the curve is!). Each step adds to the error created with the last step, and the problem thereby accumulates. Smaller step sizes minimize this problem, but the better solution is to use a better algorithm. A fourth-order Runge-Kutta is based on the Euler concept, but it produces highly accurate results. (For a more detailed discussion of the error associated with Euler's method, see Blanchard et al., 2006, pp. 627–637.)

Heun's Method

Heun's method is sometimes called an "improved Euler" method, and it is a second-order Runge-Kutta. Some readers may wonder why it is important to discuss Heun's method at all given the fact that a fourth-order Runge-Kutta method is the one that they will probably use in practice. But Heun's method is introduced here because it is more manageable to explain with the second-order case how higher-order Runge-Kutta methods work in principle. While we do not need to go into too many details here, it is worthwhile noting that the "order" of a Runge-Kutta method is related to a characteristic of its error (see Blanchard et al., 2006, pp. 646–647, as well as Zill, 2005, pp. 373–374). Even a second-order Runge-Kutta produces remarkable improvements in accuracy over Euler's method.

The basic concept of Heun's method is quite simple. With Euler's method, we used the differential equation to tell us if the values of the dependent variable are increasing or decreasing at a particular point on the curve. How much the dependent variable is increasing or decreasing depends on the value of the derivative of y, which is the differential equation itself. Heun's method works by giving us a better idea of how much to increase or decrease our dependent variable. To do this, it calculates two derivatives of y and then takes the average of these. This average is then multiplied by the step size (exactly as is done by Euler's method) in order to get the next value of y. Since Heun's method is more accurate than Euler's method, it is possible to use a larger step size, thereby increasing the efficiency (and speed) of the calculations.

More specifically, Heun's method begins with an application of Euler's method. That is, we use Euler's method to give us the next value of y based on the current value of y. This means that we are applying Euler's method to the point (t_0, y_0). We will later need the value of the derivative that we used with this application of Euler's method, so we save it and call it m. We now have the points (t_0, y_0) and (t_{next}, y_{next}), where the second point came from the application of Euler's method. Now we apply Euler's method again, but this time to the point (t_{next}, y_{next}). We will also need the value of the derivative used with this step, so we save it and call it n. Finally, we go back to our original point (t_0, y_0) and apply Euler's method once more, but this time we use the average of m and n for our derivative. Thus, we obtain our next value of y by applying the formula

$$y_{next} = y + h\left(\frac{m+n}{2}\right), \qquad [2.15]$$

where h is the step size, and $[(m+n)/2]$ is the average of the two derivatives calculated from two different values of y, the second of which was a result of using Euler's method with the original value of y.

The geometry of why Heun's method works is related to an application of the trapezoid rule for approximating areas under a curve, and interested readers can find accessible treatments of this in Blanchard et al. (2006, pp. 642–644). A different geometric explanation of why Heun's method works is that the error produced by using the first derivative (m) with the initial application of Euler's method is overcompensated for (with respect to the original starting point) by the next derivative (n) that is used with the second application of Euler's method. The average of these derivatives (m and n) produces a better predictor of the next value of y when applied as in Equation 2.15. Readers can find an accessible but more detailed discussion of this reasoning in Zill (2005, pp. 370–371). From this reasoning, it is easy to see that the use of the derivative n in Equation 2.15 acts to correct the error introduced by the use of the derivative m. This is why Heun's method is also occasionally referred to as a "predictor-corrector" method. Some readers may also note that Heun's method is analogous to the application of a second-degree Taylor series expansion of the original differential equation model (see Zill, 2005, p. 374).

The Fourth-Order Runge-Kutta Method

The fourth-order Runge-Kutta method (named after its developers, Carle Runge and Martin Kutta) is a highly accurate method of solving for first-order differential equations, and it will be the workhorse of choice in most situations. Whereas Heun's method obtains a value for the dependent variable y using an average of two slopes, a fourth-order Runge-Kutta does the same thing using a weighted average of four slopes. This method is often abbreviated as "RK4."

The mechanics of the RK4 method are quite simple, but there is greater housekeeping than with Heun's method. The most commonly used application of the RK4 method uses the following formulas:

$$y_{next} = y + (h/6)(k_1 + 2k_2 + 2k_3 + k_4),$$

where

$$k_1 = f(t, y),$$
$$k_2 = f[t + h/2, y + (h/2)k_1],$$
$$k_3 = f[t + h/2, y + (h/2)k_2],$$
$$k_4 = f[t + h, y + hk_3].$$

Note that the values of k_2 and k_3 are computed at only half of a step size from the original starting point (t_0, y_0), whereas the value of k_1 is computed from the starting point and k_4 is determined at a full step size from the starting point. A geometric interpretation of why the RK4 method works can be found in Blanchard et al. (2006, pp. 650–651). But briefly, we can see from the equations above that the value of y_{next} is computed using an approach similar to Euler's method, with the difference being that instead of using one value of the derivative, we use four, and the inner two (k_2 and k_3) are given double weights (for a total of six weights, which is why we divide by 6 to get the average). Other than the fact that we are using a weighted average of four derivatives, we are still multiplying this by the step size, h, and then adding this product to the original value of y to get the next value of y. Readers should note that in some books, the formulas for the RK4 method use the notation rk_1, rk_2, rk_3, and rk_4 instead of k_1 through k_4.

Summary

This chapter has focused on first-order differential equations. We begin with analytical solutions to linear first-order differential equations, with the emphasis on the separation of variables technique. In situations in which the separation of variables technique can successfully be applied, this is an easy and straightforward method of obtaining an equation from which one can obtain x and y values useful for plotting and analysis. In situations in which the separation of variables technique cannot be applied, we use numerical methods of integration. Among first-order differential equations, there are four "ideal types" that we explore: (1) exponential growth, (2) exponential decay, (3) learning curves and noninteractive diffusion, and (4) the logistic curve. A classic example from sociology is presented that compares types 3 and 4 above. The chapter then introduces three numerical methods for solving differential equations. The first two, Euler's and Heun's, are used to help introduce the fourth-order Runge-Kutta method, which is the method of choice for most applications. Many other numerical methods exist, but the fourth-order Runge-Kutta serves as a good starting point and a useful workhorse in most settings. Numerical methods are particularly useful because they work well in nearly all real-world situations, both linear and nonlinear. Analytical methods of indefinite integration normally do not work for most interesting nonlinear models. In highly complex (and unusual) situations in which neither analytical methods nor numerical methods can solve a differential equation, one must resort to a careful study of the equation's algebra.

Chapter 2 Appendix

To show how these formulas are used in practice, the program below (written in SAS, but easily adaptable to other languages) was used to prepare Figure 2.3 for the learning curve. It is important to show how this works with a program, since some social scientists will inevitably find themselves programming their own RK4 models. There are software packages that contain RK4 methods within them, and some scientists may find these packages useful. But other scientists may find that the packages offer insufficient flexibility for the oddities associated with particular real-life situations, and programming one's own model with an RK4 method may be required. The bright side is that once one has programmed one model with an RK4 method, it is easy to cut and paste the code into any number of other applications. Remember, with only slight modifications (e.g., step size, initial conditions, parameter values), the same code works with nearly all differential equations.

With the code below, capitalization is for style only, and whether something is capitalized or not does not affect the running of the program. There are two subroutines: RK4 and EQS. BUILDIT is a label in the program that is found below the RK4 and EQS subroutines, and the RK4 subroutine is called there. The EQS subroutine is called from within the RK4 subroutine, and it houses the differential equation model.

```
GOPTIONS lfactor=10 hsize=6 in vsize=6 in horigin=1 in
    vorigin=3 in;
TITLE f=swissb h=1.6 c=black 'Figure 2.3:  A Learning Curve';
PROC IML;
a=3.0; * The parameter value for the model;
Y=0.1;U=1.6; * The initial condition for Y, and the limit U;
h=0.02;time=0; * The step size, h, and the initial value of time;

START;
GOTO BUILDIT;

RK4:
* Fourth Order Runge-Kutta;
time=0;
DO LOOP=1 to 100;
m1=Y; * This sets the initial value of the dependent variable to Y
    for the first RK4 step;
LINK EQS; * This links the equation subroutine for the first step
    of the RK4;
RK1=DYDT; *This completes the first RK4 step;
m1=Y+(.5#h#RK1); * m1 is now given its second value that is
    used in the second RK4 step;
LINK EQS; * This links the equation subroutine for the second
    step of the RK4;
RK2=DYDT; * This completes the second RK4 step;
m1=Y+(.5#h#RK2); * m1 is now given its third value that is used
    in the third RK4 step;
LINK EQS; * This links the equation subroutine for the third step
    of the RK4;
RK3=DYDT; * This completes the third RK4 step;
m1=Y + h#RK3; * m1 is now given its fourth value that is used in
    the final RK4 step;
LINK EQS; * This links the equation subroutine for the final step
    of the RK4;
RK4=DYDT; * This completes the fourth and final RK4 step;

YNEXT=Y+((h/6)#(RK1+(2#RK2)+(2#RK3)+RK4)); * This is
    the RK4;
```

```
timenext=time+h;

YE=YE//Y;TE=TE//time; * Saving the values of Y and T in
    vectors;
trajects=YE||TE;
Y=YNEXT;time=timenext;
end; * The end of the loop;
RETURN;

* The Learning Curve Model using various values of Y as m1 for
    the four RK4 steps;
EQS:
DYDT = a#(U - m1); * This is the model;
RETURN;

BUILDIT:
LINK RK4;
party={'Y' 'Time'};
create traject from trajects (|colname=party|);
append from trajects;
close traject;
finish;run;

data traject;set traject; * This plots the results;
sym=1;
symbol1 color=black v=none f=simplex i=join;
proc gplot data=traject;
axis1 color=black minor=none order=0 to 2 by .2 minor=none
value=(h=1.5 f=swissb c=black)
label=(a=90 r=0 h=2 f=swissb c=black 'Dependent Variable');
axis2 color=black minor=none order=0 to 2 by .25 minor=none
value=(h=1.5 f=swissb c=black)
label=(h=2 f=swissb c=black 'Time');
plot Y*time=sym / skipmiss nolegend
vaxis=axis1 haxis=axis2 vminor=0 hminor=0 vref=1.6;
run;
quit;
```

3. SYSTEMS OF FIRST-ORDER
DIFFERENTIAL EQUATIONS

With single differential equations, there is only one dependent variable. But very few things in the world can be studied in isolation. It is normal for A to influence B, and for B to influence A (and perhaps C as well), and so on. For this reason, we study systems. Systems are among the most important areas in the application of differential equations. In this chapter we examine *first-order* differential equation systems. This is the most important category of differential equation systems. The reason is that higher-order and nonautonomous differential equations can be expressed in terms of first-order differential equation systems. Indeed, first-order differential equation systems are required to conduct numerical investigations of higher-order equations using, say, a fourth-order Runge-Kutta (RK4). Thus, first-order differential equation systems are exceptionally useful to the study of differential equations in general.

There are two types of first-order differential equation systems: linear and nonlinear. We can analyze linear systems using analytic, qualitative, and numerical methods. Analytic methods involve finding explicit solutions for the differential equation systems, which is analogous to how we used the separation of variables technique to solve some single differential equations in a previous chapter. However, nonlinear systems can usually only be analyzed using qualitative and numerical methods since it is rare that we can derive general and explicit solutions for most nonlinear systems. Analytic methods are still interesting to use with linear systems, however, since such methods help us understand types of behaviors for such systems, and these behaviors can be surprisingly varied. It is useful to note that nonlinear systems can behave similarly to linear systems near equilibria, and thus knowing how linear systems behave helps us understand much about nonlinear systems as well. I present material involving analytic solutions to linear systems later in this book.

Qualitative and numerical methods are of general use for investigating all differential equation systems since they are widely applicable to both linear and nonlinear systems. Also, within the social sciences, it is exceptionally common for specification nonlinearities to arise within social scientific dynamic models. For example, every time one population interacts with another population, such as when workers and nonworkers interact, there are nonlinearities in the model specification (e.g., Przeworski & Soares, 1971; see also Przeworski & Sprague, 1986 with respect to difference equations). The focus of this chapter is on qualitative and numerical methods that are used to study first-order differential equation systems.

The Predator-Prey Model

The differential equation system that is probably the most useful with respect to introducing the basic concepts of first-order differential equations systems is the predator-prey model of Lotka and Volterra (see Hirsch & Smale, 1974, pp. 258–265; Koçak, 1989, pp. 121–122; May, 1974). While the model arises out of population biology, its linear and nonlinear components have been widely used in many social scientific settings, and readers are encouraged to study it closely. To introduce this model, I will stick to its population biology interpretation, although I will later extend the discussion of the model's components to human social examples.

The basic idea with the predator-prey system is that there are two populations, one of which preys upon the other. Using a real-life example, in the presence of food, rabbits breed new rabbits, and the rabbit population grows. As the rabbit population grows, there is more food for foxes to eat. This causes the fox population to grow. Eventually, there are so many foxes that the rabbit population begins to decline in numbers. This results in having many foxes die due to starvation and hardship. When the fox population diminishes, there is little to restrain the rabbit population, so the rabbits again grow in numbers, the fox population follows, and the cycle repeats itself.

This is an example of a closed system, in the sense that everything that affects the system is contained in the system. There are no external factors that influence the fox and rabbit populations. Some theorists also call this an "isolated system." In the physical sciences, the terms "closed system" and "isolated system" differ somewhat. For example, a closed system can exchange heat and work from outside of its boundaries, while an isolated system cannot. Neither type can exchange matter. But these distinctions do not affect us here, and in the current context the terms can be used interchangeably. An open system is one in which external factors can affect the dynamics of the variables, and in this case, populations could rise or fall because of these factors.

If we identify the rabbit population with the letter X and the fox population with the letter Y, we can express this predator-prey relationship as in Equations 3.1 and 3.2,

$$dX/dt = aX - bXY - mX^2, \qquad [3.1]$$

$$dY/dt = cXY - eY - nY^2, \qquad [3.2]$$

where a, b, m, c, e, and n are constant parameters. These two equations form an interdependent system of two first-order nonlinear differential equations.

They are nonlinear because of the interactive and power terms (e.g., XY, X^2, and Y^2) in both equations. They are interdependent because the variables X and Y appear in both equations, which means that dY/dt depends on both X and Y, as does dX/dt. These are the more generalized versions of the classic predator-prey equations of Lotka (1925) and Volterra (1930, 1931). Less general versions of these equations set the parameters m and n to zero, which I explain further below.

Both X and Y depend on time in the above representation. In the classic predator-prey scenario, the number of rabbits increases exponentially (aX) until they are either eaten by the foxes ($-bXY$) or their population rises to its limit due to limitations in food resources ($-mX^2$). The population of foxes grows only when there are rabbits to eat (cXY). Fox populations decline due to natural causes ($-eY$) or due to their own crowding and overexploitation of their available resources ($-nY^2$).

It is worthwhile noting commonalities between the specification of the predator-prey model and the logistic model described earlier as Equation 2.8. In the absence of foxes, Equation 3.1 could have been rewritten as

$$dX/dt = X(a - mX). \qquad [3.3]$$

The connection between Equation 3.3 and Equation 2.8 can be found in the following algebra:

$$dX/dt = aX[1 - (m/a)X],$$
$$dX/dt = a(m/a)X[a/m - X],$$
$$dX/dt = mX[U - X],$$

where $U = a/m$. However, the full predator-prey model adds interaction between the two species via the multiplicative term XY, and this is its primary departure from the single-equation logistic model.

Note also that in Equation 3.3, there is a logistic limit of a/m. This is found by setting the Equation 3.3 equal to zero (which is what the derivative equals when X is at its limit) and then solving for X. Similarly, in the absence of rabbits, Equation 3.2 shows that the limit for the fox population is zero (since growth can only occur in the presence of rabbits). These are also called "equilibrium values" of the dependent variables, which I discuss more thoroughly below.

The predator-prey model is often introduced without the crowding and resource limitation terms (mX^2 and nY^2) found in Equations 3.1 and 3.2 to show how the population interactions work by themselves. One way to represent the interactions between these two variables is with a time series plot, as is done in Figure 3.1. In this figure, the scale of the vertical axis is

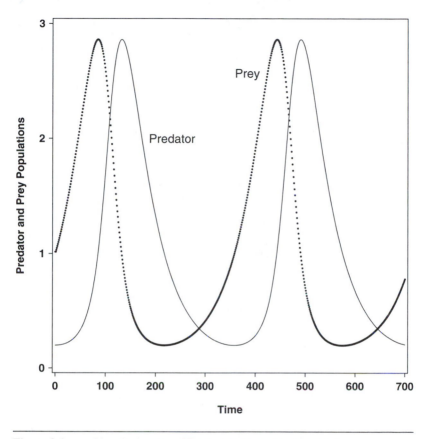

Figure 3.1   Time Series Plot of Predator-Prey Model Without Resource
Limitations

arbitrary, and one can think of the numbers more realistically in terms of
hundreds. To create this plot, the parameters m and n are set equal to zero.
Note here that the fox population "chases" the rabbit population in terms
of overall quantities, there being a lag as the number of foxes adjusts to
changes in the number of rabbits.

The time series plot takes on a distinctly different character for the full
predator-prey model that includes the crowding and resource limitation
terms (mX^2 and nY^2). Such a plot is presented as Figure 3.2. Note that the
time series for both the predator and prey populations settle down at equilibrium values, which we can identify throughout this book using the notation (X^*, Y^*).

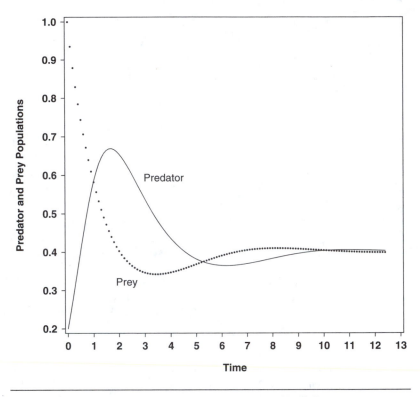

Figure 3.2   Time Series Plot of Predator-Prey Model With Resource Limitations

The Phase Diagram

It is common when working with systems of differential equations to want to know how one variable changes with respect to another variable. In this sense, time gets in the way. We can eliminate time from the analysis by dividing Equation 3.1 by Equation 3.2, as is done with Equation 3.4.

$$\frac{dX}{dY} = \frac{aX - bXY - mX^2}{cXY - eY - nY^2} \qquad [3.4]$$

Various analytics can be accomplished using Equation 3.4, but more generally we use a set of graphical techniques that allows us to investigate the joint behaviors of the system variables in the absence of a time axis. The most basic of such techniques is a "phase portrait" (or "phase diagram")

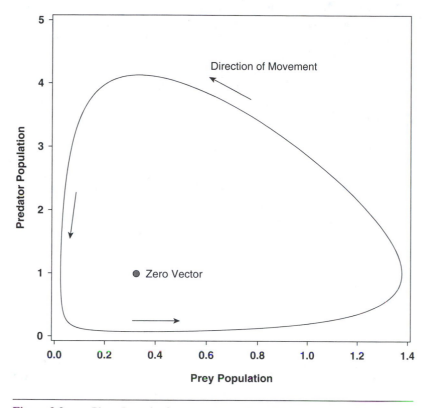

Figure 3.3   Phase Portrait of Predator-Prey Model Without Resource Limitations

of the system. We use phase portraits to portray graphically the sequential dynamics of the variables X and Y while suppressing time. One such phase portrait of this system is presented as Figure 3.3. Figure 3.3 corresponds with Figure 3.1, in the sense that the parameters n and m are set to zero. This is a situation in which there are no crowding and resource limitations.

In Figure 3.3, note that the time axis no longer exists. Rather, we now have a representation of the sequential changes in X and Y independent of time. The elliptical curve in the figure is called a "trajectory," and this trajectory is located in the "phase space" (i.e., the dimensions absent time) of this system with two variables. If time were to be included, a third axis would be required that would project off the page toward the reader's face. The trajectory would then spiral outward from the page in the manner of a rocket's smoke trail rather than remain as in Figure 3.3 as a curve on a flat surface.

Note the oscillatory nature of the trajectory in Figure 3.3. The placement and size of the elliptical orbit of the trajectory is determined by the initial condition, which in this case is $(X_0, Y_0) = (1, 0.2)$. With only one exception, wherever one starts in this system, an elliptical orbit will result as the predator and prey populations cycle indefinitely following the exact same path with each orbit. This, of course, assumes a purely deterministic world, which we never have. Stochasticity will introduce variations in this path, but the general cyclical nature of the underlying deterministic system will persevere.

Equilibria Within Phase Diagrams

The one exception to the pattern of elliptical orbits as shown in Figure 3.3 is at a point called the "equilibrium." An equilibrium point is where change in the dependent variables ceases to exist. This is where the derivatives (Equations 3.1 and 3.2) are equal to zero.

In Figure 3.3, the equilibrium is located somewhere in the center of the elliptical orbit of the trajectory, and its X and Y coordinates are obtained by solving the two equations simultaneously. Since the parameters m and n are equal to zero for the situation found in Figure 3.3, we have

$$0 = aX - bXY,$$
$$0 = cXY - eY.$$

This produces the formulas $(X^*, Y^*) = (e/c, a/b)$. This type of equilibrium that resides inside of an elliptical trajectory is called a "center," and it is stable (a quality that I discuss below). To produce Figure 3.3, I set the parameters equal to the following values: $a = 1, b = 1, c = 3, e = 1$. Thus, the equilibrium for this system is $(1/3, 1)$. There is also another equilibrium at $(0, 0)$, but this point is boring.

Aside from determining the specification of the original model, the two most important things to do with any differential equation system are (1) to determine the equilibria for the system and (2) determine if the equilibria are stable or unstable. The system presented in Figure 3.3 clearly has an equilibrium value, so we have accomplished our first objective. For the second objective, we note that an unstable equilibrium acts to repel trajectories away from it. The repelling movement can be slight, as in a slow drifting away from the equilibrium, or more rapid. But if the trajectories near an equilibrium do not drift way from it over time, then the equilibrium is stable. Some stable equilibria can be attractors while others can be neutral. An attracting equilibrium draws trajectories in phase space toward itself. A neutral equilibrium neither attracts nor repels trajectories, and the vector $(X^*, Y^*) = (e/c, a/b)$ in Figure 3.3 is neutral. If the initial condition for the

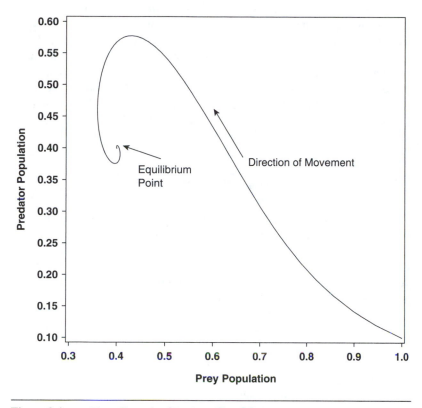

Figure 3.4   Phase Portrait of Predator-Prey Model With Resource Limitations

---

system shown in Figure 3.3 were to be placed exactly on the point (e/c, a/b), then the system would not vary, and the values would stay fixed on that point forever. But any stochastic movement off that point would result in oscillations of the type described above. Since the oscillations would not drift systematically and continually away from the equilibrium, the equilibrium is stable.

If we reintroduce the crowding and resource limitation terms for the predator-prey model by setting the parameters m and n to nonzero values, then the qualitative characteristic of the equilibrium changes to become both stable and attracting. This can be seen in the phase portrait shown in Figure 3.4. In this figure, note that the trajectory begins in the lower right corner of the figure and then follows a curving path that both circles and gets closer to the equilibrium point. The area within phase space that falls under the attracting influence of a stable equilibrium is called the "basin" of the attractor. In this figure, all of the visible phase area falls within the basin of the attractor. To produce Figure 3.4, I set the values of the parameters as follows: $a = 1$, $b = 1$, $c = 3$; $e = 1$, $m = 1.5$, $n = 0.5$, with the initial conditions $X = 1$ and $Y = 0.1$. The equilibrium value of this system is found by setting Equations 3.1 and 3.2 equal to zero and then solving the set of simultaneous equations for the values of X^* and Y^*. Here, $X^* = (eb + an)/(cb + mn)$, and $Y^* = (ca - em)/(bc + mn)$, which is the equilibrium for this system. In the example given in Figure 3.4, $(X^*, Y^*) = (0.4, 0.4)$.

Vector Field and Direction Field Diagrams

While a phase portrait as shown in Figures 3.3 and 3.4 is useful in showing how one or more trajectories move through a model's phase space, one can always wonder where a trajectory might have gone had it passed through a different area in the phase space. One way to answer this question is with a vector field diagram or a direction field diagram. The two types of diagrams are closely related. To create a vector field diagram of a two-dimensional system, one establishes a grid of points within the area of interest. In terms of theory, you obtain the slope of the line (dX/dY) that intersects each of the points in the grid. This slope is the same as Equation 3.4 for the predator-prey model discussed above. Then you draw a line (often with an arrow-head) that begins on each grid point and goes in the direction of the slope for each respective point. The length of the line is dependent on the values of the system equations at any selected point in the phase space, and it is the magnitude of the vector $\mathbf{V}(dX/dt, dY/dt)$.

In practical terms with respect to actually plotting a vector field, each vector has two components, dX/dt and dY/dt. These derivatives evaluated at each grid point are your displacement values that you use to move the vector on your graph from each of the grid points to an end point for each vector. To get the end points for each vector, you do the following: (1) substitute into dX/dt and dY/dt the values of X and Y for each grid point that is selected for the vector diagram, (2) calculate the values of dX/dt and dY/dt, and then (3) add these values to the X and Y points for each grid point. The grid points are your starting values for your vectors, and the end points of the vectors are the original starting values plus the displacement values. One then draws the vectors in the vector field by connecting the starting grid points with the ending points. You show direction either by putting an arrowhead on the end of each line or by placing a large dot on the beginning of each line.

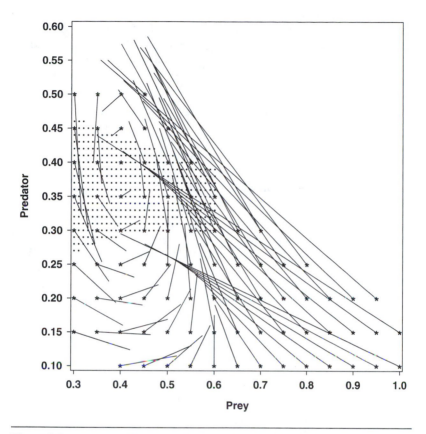

Figure 3.5 Vector Diagram of Predator-Prey Model With Resource Limitations

An example of a vector field diagram for the predator-prey model with growth and crowding limitations is presented in Figure 3.5. While I programmed SAS to produce Figure 3.5, programs exist that can do all of this for you. Here also Phaser is an exceptionally useful program for creating graphics of the type presented in Figure 3.5 (www.phaser.com). Phaser is a program that I often use in my modeling classes. It produces phase diagrams, vector field diagrams, and direction field diagrams as well as many other tools for graphical analysis. Moreover, it produces these things in real time so that students can watch the construction of the diagrams (i.e., "live") as they are projected onto a screen by a data projector.

When constructing vector diagrams, it is often necessary to scale the length of the vectors so that they are not too long. In Figure 3.5, I did not use a scaling factor that works by multiplying each of the displacements by a proportion less than 1 (0.45 is often a useful number to try). Because I did not use a scaling factor when producing Figure 3.5, some of the displacements are exceptionally large, and some are so large that they were not even printed in the figure. This is the reason why the upper-right corner of the figure is empty; all of those vectors traveled outside of the box containing the figure. Also, in Figure 3.5 I did not put arrowheads at the ends of the lines because the arrowheads made the graph too "messy," in the sense that there was just too much ink on the page to make sense of what was going on. In this instance, the arrowheads are not needed since the grid points are visible (as asterisks), and the vectors travel away from the grid points. Nonetheless, even without the arrowheads, this graph is still too messy. The great thing about vector diagrams is that you can get a sense of how "fast" a trajectory will travel in an area of the phase space by looking at the length of the vectors in that area. But this extra information comes at a steep price. The vectors tend to cross over one another, and it often becomes difficult to sort things out. For this reason, direction field diagrams are sometimes used instead of vector field diagrams. Note also that there is an area of small dots in Figure 3.5, and that is an "equilibrium marsh" as I explain below.

Direction field diagrams solve the problem of having vectors cross over one another by scaling the vectors such that they all have the same (short) length. This allows one to see the direction that a trajectory would take if it passed through a point in phase space, although we now do not have an idea of how fast that trajectory would be traveling. Because of the greater ease of reading such graphs, direction field diagrams are often preferred over vector field diagrams. Figure 3.6 is an example of a direction field diagram. Here, the direction indicators are shorter than those shown in Figure 3.5, and the lengths are obtained by dividing both the X and Y displacements (which are the derivatives themselves) by a scaling factor. The formula for the scaling factor is

$$\text{scaling factor} = \sqrt{\frac{(dX/dt)^2 + (dY/dt)^2}{\text{length}}},$$

where the length is how long you want the direction vectors to appear on the graph.

As with vector field diagrams, readers are encouraged to use software such as Phaser to construct direction field diagrams, especially for exploratory purposes. Phaser does all of the plotting and scaling for you. Nonetheless, it helps to know how to do this for yourself should you encounter

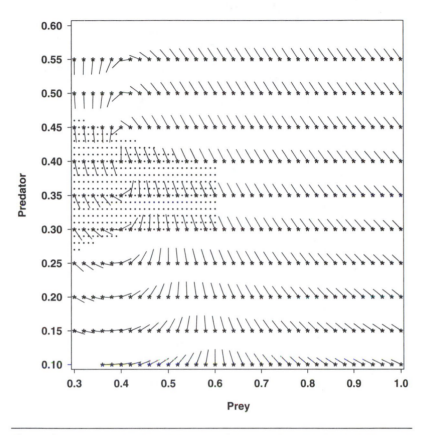

Figure 3.6   Direction Field Diagram of Predator-Prey Model With Resource Limitations

unique situations related to your particular model that require you to program your own direction field diagrams. Indeed, I often find that I need to construct plots that address special conditions that cannot be resolved using any of the available software graphing packages. For example, in Figure 3.7, I present a previously published vector field diagram that has two unique characteristics. The model upon which the vector field diagram is based describes the landslide election in the United States between Johnson and Goldwater in 1964 (see Brown 1995a, p. 73; also 1993). Figure 3.7 is for areas outside of the deep southern states. Since the proportions of the Democratic and Republican votes cannot sum to be greater than unity, I had to be sure to eliminate any direction indicators in the upper right-hand corner

52

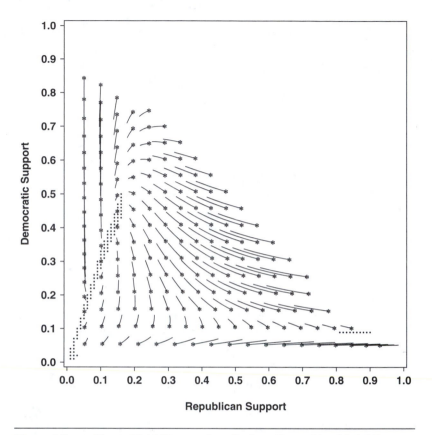

Figure 3.7   Vector Field Diagram for a Partisan Competition Model Between Democratic and Republican Parties in Nonsouthern Areas of the United States, 1964

of the graph, which could not be easily accomplished with prepackaged software.

Note also in Figure 3.7 that the direction indicators differ from those typical of traditional vector field or direction field diagrams. It is my preference sometimes to use six iterations (or some similarly small number) of an RK4 method to plot the direction field indicators rather than to use the derivatives directly to create the displacements. The result is that the direction indicators display some curvature to them rather than being straight, and this is more artistically pleasing to me. Also, this curving quality resolves the problem with traditional vector field diagrams of having the vectors cross over one another. This allows the direction indicators to have varying lengths, thereby retaining the trajectory speed information available with traditional vector field diagrams. This is a richer approach to vector field diagrams, although it does require additional programming. Users of such methods will need to decide for themselves which methods are most appropriate for their own particular applications.

The Equilibrium Marsh and Flow Diagrams

Now I can address those patterns of dots that appear in Figures 3.5, 3.6, and 3.7. Each of those dotted areas is an "equilibrium marsh." Equilibrium marshes are not commonly encountered in traditional studies of differential equations, but they are important in many social scientific applications of differential equations. In applications of differential equations that are commonly encountered in the physical and natural sciences, the focus is on the equilibria themselves and on the behaviors of trajectories near those equilibria. That is because such systems have the ability to run sufficiently long (and with sufficiently higher frequencies) such that the systems have a chance to settle down at or near the relevant equilibria. However, social systems move much slower than, say, an electronically driven harmonic oscillator. Social scientists often study systems that begin, grow, and expire before any really discernable behavior at or near an equilibrium can be discerned.

To put the problem in the context of an example, let us say we are studying an electoral competition. The election begins and ends within the span of a few months. We do not have a situation similar to that of a physical scientist who has the luxury of being able to watch, say, a pendulum swing back and forth for hundreds or thousands of cycles. Indeed, social systems may end before the trajectories arrive at anywhere near an equilibrium. For example, when elections take place, tracking polls watch the changing preferences of the voters on a daily basis. In many elections it is not uncommon for someone to observe, based on how the tracking polls had been moving, that a different candidate or party might have won an election had the election been postponed a few weeks, or, in really close elections, days. Sometimes a social system can be in equilibrium, but sometimes a social or political event occurs that simply interrupts or terminates a dynamic process that was not yet at or near equilibrium. What often happens in such situations is that trajectories slow down when they approach equilibria. Thus, in many social scientific situations, we need to know not only where the equilibria are located, but also where the areas exist in phase space in which change slows down to a crawl. These areas are equilibrium marshes.

They are important to social scientists because it is likely that trajectories in phase space will terminate within those equilibrium marshes rather than at equilibria. Equilibria are found within equilibrium marshes, but trajectories of social phenomena are likely to get "stuck" and terminate inside the marshes before arriving at or even near the equilibria themselves.

Equilibrium marshes are calculated by evaluating the magnitudes (i.e., the absolute values) of the derivatives of the system, which are, of course, the differential equations themselves. For example, in a two-dimensional system, when the magnitudes of *both* derivatives, dX/dt and dY/dt, are below some specified sensitivity level, then that area in the phase space is identified as an equilibrium marsh. In such areas, change in both of the variables is so slight that it is likely that the social system will terminate or be interrupted before progressing much further. The sensitivity level is arbitrary and needs to be adjusted experimentally on a case-by-case basis, depending largely on how long the system is allowed to progress before it is terminated or interrupted. However, useful starting values are typically between 0.1 and 0.01.

There is another type of plot that is similar to Figure 3.7 that can be used to show in a realistic fashion how the model's trajectories actually look with respect to data. Since the trajectories for social scientific studies may not progress all the way to an equilibrium, it is normal to ask just how far they really do progress. The actual length of a trajectory will be determined by the step size and the number of iterations used for the RK4 method. These are established when one is estimating the model's parameters with respect to data, and a discussion of how this is done can be found in Brown (1995a, see especially the appendix). Once one has the parameter values for a differential equation model, it is useful to create a "flow diagram" that presents the paths of a number of trajectories in phase space. Each of the trajectories is given a realistic initial condition and is allowed to travel only as long as would be allowed by the estimation program that determined the values of the parameters. The actual initial conditions for this plot can be randomly chosen as long as the values are realistic of the data encountered in the study. An example of such a flow diagram is presented in Figure 3.8 (see also Brown 1995a, p. 75). This flow diagram corresponds with the same model and parameter values as with Figure 3.7. Readers should note that the program Phaser (again, www.phaser.com) can also draw flow diagrams with point and click ease, although I programmed Figure 3.8 myself using SAS.

Also, it is important to note that flow diagrams can be made without restricting the length of the trajectories. One can let the trajectories proceed all the way to a close neighborhood surrounding the equilibria, and indeed this heuristically useful approach is the normal way of making flow

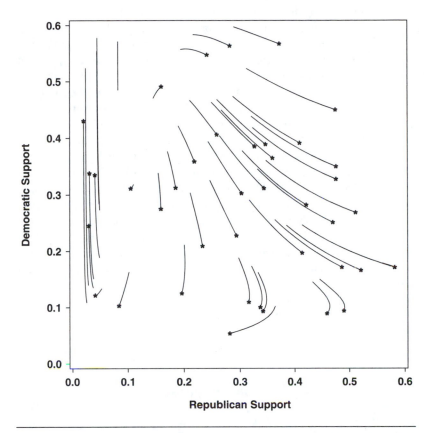

Figure 3.8   A Flow Diagram for a Partisan Competition Model Using Randomly
Chosen Initial Conditions Within Reasonable Ranges

diagrams. But flow diagrams can also be exceptionally useful in realistically
showing how the data behave within a system. When a system is interrupted
due to, say, an electoral calendar, a revolution, an assassination, or whatever,
reproducing truncated flows in a phase portrait helps to portray the extent of
the system's influence on the data.

Summary

This chapter introduces systems of differential equations. Most researchers
will want to work with systems rather than single equation models since this

is where the real power of differential equation modeling becomes apparent. The primary emphasis in this chapter is on using graphical techniques to analyze systems of differential equations. The primary graphical technique is the phase diagram, which is a plot of sequential variable values with the time axis suppressed. With most phase diagrams, it is normal to place system equilibria within the diagrams, and then to give examples of trajectories that flow through the phase space. The chapter then introduces the classic predator-prey model that originates from the field of population biology. Elements of this model can be found in many systems in a wide variety of fields, including the social sciences. Additional graphical techniques are introduced to analyze differential equation systems, such as vector field and direction field diagrams, with direction field diagrams often being the preferred approach due to their inherent advantage in neatness. Especially with social science topics in which change is slow, differential equation systems often do not have a chance to evolve to the point where the system trajectories actually arrive at an equilibrium. In reality, the trajectories "bog down" when they pass anywhere near the equilibrium in what is called an "equilibrium marsh." Placing the equilibrium marshes in the phase diagram is a useful way to identify those areas where trajectory velocity is so slow that the system essentially comes to a near halt even though equilibrium has not been achieved.

Chapter 3 Appendix

Below is a program written in SAS that uses an RK4 method with a system of two equations. Readers should note how easy it is to extend the program for a single differential equation as presented in the appendix for Chapter 2 to a system of equations as done below. This particular program was used to produce Figure 3.2 in this book. This program can also be adapted easily to produce a phase diagram such as Figure 3.4, as I explain at the end of this appendix. The RK4 algorithm can be understood using the comment statements found in the appendix to Chapter 2.

```
GOPTIONS lfactor=10 hsize=6 in vsize=6 in horigin=1 in
    vorigin=3 in;
TITLE f=swissb h=1.6 c=black 'Figure 3.2: The Predator-Prey
    Model';
PROC IML;
```

```
a=1;b=1; c=3; e=1; m=1.5; n=0.5;
X=1;Y= 0.2;
h=0.1;time=0; * The step size, h, and the initial value of time;
start;
goto buildit;

RK4:
*  Fourth-Order Runge-Kutta;
time=0;
do LOOP=1 to 125;
x1=X;x2=Y;
LINK EQS;
RK1=DXDT;CK1=DYDT;
x1=X+(.5#h#RK1);x2=Y+(.5#h#CK1);
LINK EQS;
RK2=DXDT;CK2=DYDT;
x1=X+(.5#h#RK2);x2=Y+(.5#h#CK2);
LINK EQS;
RK3=DXDT;CK3=DYDT;
x1=X + (h#RK3);x2=Y + (h#CK3);
LINK EQS;
RK4=DXDT;CK4=DYDT;

XNEXT=X+((h/6)#(RK1+(2#RK2)+(2#RK3)+RK4));
YNEXT=Y+((h/6)#(CK1+(2#CK2)+(2#CK3)+CK4));
timenext=time+h;

YE=YE//Y;XE=XE//X;TE=TE//time;
trajects=XE||(YE||TE);
Y=YNEXT;X=XNEXT;time=timenext;
end;
RETURN;

* The Predator-Prey Model;
EQS:
DXDT =(a - b#x2 - m#x1)#x1;
DYDT =(c#x1 - e - n#x2)#x2;
RETURN;

BUILDIT:
```

58

```
LINK RK4;
party={'X' 'Y' 'Time'};
create traject from trajects (|colname=party|);
append from trajects;
close traject;
finish;run;

data traject;set traject;
sym=1;
if t=0 then sym=3;
label Y='Predator and Prey Populations';
label t='Time';
symbol1 color=black v=NONE f=centb i=join;
symbol2 color=black f=centb v='.';

proc gplot data=traject;
axis1 color=black minor=none
value=(h=1.5 f=swissb c=black)
label=(h=1.3 a=90 r=0 f=swissb c=black);
axis2 color=black minor=none
value=(h=1.5 f=swissb c=black)
label=(h=1.3 f=swissb c=black);
plot Y*Time X*Time / overlay nolegend skipmiss
vaxis=axis1 haxis=axis2 vminor=0 hminor=0;
run;
quit;
```

To change this program so that it produces a phase diagram such as
Figure 3.4, simply change the plot statements at the end. For example,
to produce Figure 3.4, replace the end of the above program with the
following:

```
data traject;set traject;
sym=1;
if t=0 then sym=3;
label Y='Predator Population';
```

```
label X='Prey Population';
label t='Time';
symbol1 color=black v=NONE f=centb i=join;
symbol2 color=black f=centb v='.';

proc gplot data=traject;
axis1 color=black minor=none
value=(h=1.5 f=swissb c=black)
label=(h=1.3 a=90 r=0 f=swissb c=black);
axis2 color=black minor=none
value=(h=1.5 f=swissb c=black)
label=(h=1.3 f=swissb c=black);
plot Y*X / nolegend skipmiss
vaxis=axis1 haxis=axis2 vminor=0 hminor=0;
run;
quit;
```

4. SOME CLASSIC SOCIAL SCIENCE
EXAMPLES OF FIRST-ORDER SYSTEMS

At this point, it is most useful to introduce a number of classic differential equation systems that have made a significant impact in the social sciences. Readers will find that many aspects of these systems have parallels with parts of the predator-prey model described previously. The discussion below will lead naturally to additional methods for analyzing such systems.

More specifically, three classic models are introduced that have been very influential in the more general development and application of differential equations in the social sciences. They are (1) Richardson's (1960) arms race model, three scenarios of Lanchester's (1916) combat model, and Rapoport's (1960) production and exchange model. Studying these models closely allows us to more fully understand the underlying processes that are captured in the models. We can also run simulations with the models to test "what if?" ideas that could tell us more about the dynamics of the processes. Some of these explorations can increase our predictive understanding with respect to these processes. If we are modeling things that we do not want to happen in real life, such as a run-away arms race or catastrophic global warming, then extrapolating from our models can be crucial in terms of learning how to manage our world more effectively. Indeed, to this day many militaries use Lanchester's combat model to simulate various battlefield scenarios before committing their troops. Simulation is one of the great benefits of modeling in general.

The use of differential equation modeling is not a panacea for any application. All models are simplifications of reality. Sometimes simple ordinary least squares (OLS) regression models are all we need for a given situation. But quite often, the complexity of a dynamic process is only fully revealed in the context of its more accurate specification with respect to time. In such situations, using differential equations allows us to approximate more closely the actual continuous-time processes such that we can make the most out of our explorations and extrapolations. The three models presented below are excellent examples of such an appropriate use of differential equation modeling.

Richardson's Arms Race Model

The arms race model of Lewis F. Richardson is without doubt among the most deservedly famous of differential equation models in the social sciences. A great deal has been written about Richardson's ideas and his models, and it is not possible here to reference that huge literature. But the basic arms race model itself is still of fundamental importance to the study of arms races and to society more generally. Indeed, Richardson himself seems to have believed that his perceptions relating to the way nations compete militarily might have been useful in preventing the outbreak of hostilities in World War II (see Richardson, 1960, Preface, p. ix). The model itself—a system of two interdependent differential equations—is quite simple, and it is possible to manipulate the equations analytically in order to obtain many useful results. However, I do little of this here since these manipulations are not particularly useful with other more complicated models. Rather, I focus here on methods of analysis that are generally useful to the entire class of systems of ordinary differential equations.

There are three basic premises underlying Richardson's arms race model (see Richardson, 1960, pp. 13–16). The first is that a nation spends more on weapons when it observes that other nations are spending more on weapons. However, military spending is an economic burden to society, and greater levels of spending will inhibit future increases in spending, which is the second premise. Finally, there are grievances and ambitions relating to both cultures and national leaders that either encourage or discourage changes in military spending. All of this can be summarized algebraically as

$$dx/dt = ay - mx + g, \qquad [4.1]$$
$$dy/dt = bx - ny + h. \qquad [4.2]$$

Here we have two nations, X and Y. Changes in their respective spending on arms is represented by dx/dt and dy/dt. The positive terms ay and bx represent the drive to spend more on arms due to the level of spending of the other nation, and the negative terms mx and ny reflect a nation's desire to inhibit future military spending because of the economic burden of its own current spending. The constants g and h represent the grievances and ambitions of the leaders for nations X and Y, respectively.

This is a system of two *linear* interdependent equations. The system's linearity is what makes it so easy to manipulate algebraically. Some of this manipulation is useful to reinterpret the meaning of the parameters themselves. For example, we could say that Equation 4.1 is actually measuring the imbalance between the spending levels x and y. Note that $ay - mx = a(y - mx/a)$, and we can say that the parameter a now represents a more generalized rate of military spending with respect to this balance. The parameter grouping m/a is itself a constant which acts to establish the desired level of balance (see Danby, 1997, p. 48).

As with most systems of differential equations, the first thing we want to determine is if there is an equilibrium (or multiple equilibria). We determine this by setting the differential equations (Equations 4.1 and 4.2) to zero and solving for X^* and Y^*. Here we have the equations of two lines,

$$0 = ay - mx + g, \qquad [4.3]$$
$$0 = bx - ny + h, \qquad [4.4]$$

and the equilibrium is the intersection of the two lines. In this case, $X^* = (ah + gn)/(mn - ab)$ and $Y^* = (bg + hm)/(mn - ab)$. This equilibrium exists as long as $mn - ab \neq 0$.

The next thing we want to know is if the equilibrium is stable. That is, do trajectories that exist in the neighborhood of (X^*, Y^*) flow toward the equilibrium and stay in that neighborhood, or are they repelled away from the equilibrium? The answer to this depends on the values of the parameters. One way to determine whether the equilibrium is stable for any particular set of parameter values is to draw the two lines (Equations 4.3 and 4.4) on a graph and then to note the signs of the derivatives in the various sectors of the graph as they are determined by the two lines. This has been usefully demonstrated by Richardson (1960, pp. 24–27), Danby (1997, pp. 49–50), and others.

However, stability of a two-dimensional system of first-order differential equations is explicitly connected to the stability of a second-order differential equation, and it is useful at this point to show why this is true. Later in this book, I demonstrate how to change a second-order differential equation into a system of two first-order differential equations. But it also works in the reverse, and we can rephrase a system of two first-order differential equations in terms of one second-order differential equation. In terms of the Richardson arms race model, begin with Equation 4.1 and differentiate it to obtain d^2x/dt^2. Thus, we have

$$d^2x/dt^2 = a(dy/dt) - m(dx/dt). \quad [4.5]$$

Now, substitute Equation 4.2 for dy/dt in Equation 4.5 to obtain

$$d^2x/dt^2 = a(bx - ny + h) - m(dx/dt). \quad [4.6]$$

The next step is to isolate y in Equation 4.1 and substitute this into Equation 4.6. After rearranging, you have the second-order differential equation.

$$d^2x/dt^2 + (m + n)(dx/dt) + (mn - ab)x - (ah + ng) = 0$$

In general, we do not need to transform systems of first-order differential equations into second-order differential equations to analyze them. In fact, the situation is the reverse. We need to transform second-order differential equations into systems of first-order equations to use the methods of analysis presented in this book. Nonetheless, the demonstration above is necessary on the level of understanding to show that we truly are working with higher-order differential equations when we work with systems of first-order differential equations. Second-order differential equations can "do more" than first-order differential equations, in the sense that the behaviors that second-order differential equations can exhibit are more varied than those that are possible for first-order differential equations. Thus, when we work with systems of first-order differential equations, we are purchasing all of the behavioral "power" of second-order differential equations.

Richardson's arms race model is capable of producing a remarkably varied set of behaviors. We can see these by using flow diagrams. Figure 4.1 is a combination of a flow diagram and a direction field diagram. In this instance, I used the program Phaser to construct this plot as well as some additional figures shown below. The equations together with the parameter values that are used for this figure are $dx/dt = 0.1y - 0.1x + 0.02$ and $dy/dt = 0.1x - 0.1y + 0.03$. With this set of parameters, there is a fairly equal level of distrust of the opposing nation (i.e., $a = 0.1$ and $b = 0.1$) and economic burden ($m = 0.1$ and $n = 0.1$), but the historical and leadership factors of nation Y ($h = 0.03$) are slightly more exacerbated as compared

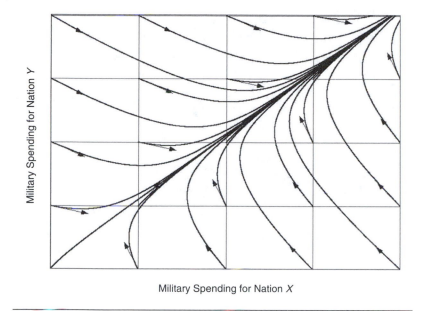

Military Spending for Nation X

Figure 4.1   Richardson's Arms Race, Scenario One

with those of nation X ($g = 0.02$). Figure 4.1 can be a terrifying scenario since what we have is a runaway arms race for both nations.

A different scenario can be seen in Figure 4.2. Here the equations are $dx/dt = y - 2x + 3$ and $dy/dt = 4x - 5y + 6$. In this instance, I am using parameter values suggested by Danby (1997, p. 51). Here it is clear that we have a stable equilibrium point near the center of the graph since all trajectories move toward this point. Another way to say this is that all of the trajectories fall within the basin of this attractor. This is an arms race that finds a balance of power.

Changing the parameter values even slightly can produce a remarkably different outcome, however, as is shown in Figure 4.3. For Figure 4.3, the equations are $dx/dt = 2y - x - 1$ and $dy/dt = 5x - 4y - 1$. With this scenario, the equilibrium point in the lower left corner of the graph is unstable, which means that it is a repeller. Trajectories eventually flow away from it, either safely toward zero or catastrophically upward without end. Which way one ends up depends on where one starts, and this is hardly a comforting situation. Of the three scenarios shown here, only Scenario Two portrayed in Figure 4.2 offers any significant real comfort. But note that to move from the relative stability of Scenario Two to the repelling

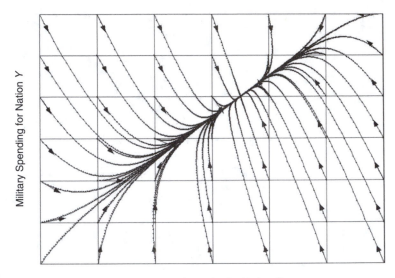

Military Spending for Nation Y

Military Spending for Nation X

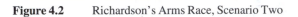

Figure 4.2   Richardson's Arms Race, Scenario Two

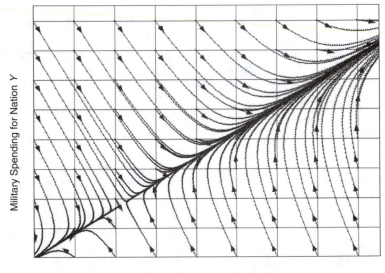

Military Spending for Nation Y

Military Spending for Nation X

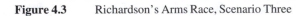

Figure 4.3   Richardson's Arms Race, Scenario Three

instability of Scenario Three (Figure 4.3) required only leadership changes (parameters h and g) with respect to the model. It is this lesson that apparently worried Richardson so much.

Much more could be written (and has been written) about Richardson's arms race model. As a starting point, some readers may find the discussions of this model by Rapoport (1960), Braun (1983), Danby (1997), and Huckfeldt, Kohfeld, and Likens (1982) to be useful. But the outline of the basic ideas above demonstrates how social scientists can use even simple differential equation models to extract from them sometimes profound lessons about human society.

Lanchester's Combat Models

F. W. Lanchester published in 1916 a collection of differential equation models that described quantitatively how various types of armies interact on the battlefield with respect to their relative troop gains and losses. The models eventually became classics, and they are still studied closely (with extensions) in general modeling courses as well as in courses involving analyses of military combat operations. Readers can find interesting treatments of these models in Braun (1983) as well as Danby (1997, pp. 139–140). A discussion of a famous application of these models to the battle of Iwo Jima during World War II can be found in Braun (1983) as well as Engel (1954).

Three scenarios are normally considered with respect to Lanchester's combat models. The variations between these models depend on whether the combatants are members of conventional or guerilla armies. The military strength of the two armies are identified using the variables x and y. There are two types of loss rates for both armies and one source of gain (from reinforcement). The first loss rate is *operational*. Operational losses occur simply as a result of having one's own army deployed. Such losses include deaths due to traffic accidents, accidental aircraft crashes, disease, and desertion. An army's operational loss rate is proportional to the number of troops that are deployed by this same army. This type of loss is identical across all three scenarios of Lanchester's combat models.

The second loss rate is *combat*. Combat losses are deaths due to the killing activities of the enemy army. When an army comprises conventional forces, then its members are visible to the enemy combatants (or out in the open). Also, conventional forces are assumed to be within the killing range of the opposing forces. Combat losses for conventional forces are proportional to the total number of enemy combatants. For example, if army X is a conventional force, then its combat loss rate would be ay, where y is the number of enemy combatants, and the parameter a is the coefficient of proportionality. This parameter is called army Y's "combat effectiveness coefficient." The higher the value of this parameter, the more effective army Y is at killing members of army X.

Combat losses for guerilla armies are different from those of conventional armies. Members of guerilla armies hide within either urban or natural environments and are not easily visible to the members of the opposing forces. To kill members of a guerilla army typically requires that the opposing army physically engage the guerilla forces either one-on-one or in small groups. Thus, personal interaction with such forces is required. Mathematically, this type of interaction is normally accomplished by multiplying the two variables, x and y, together. In this case, if army X is a guerilla army, then its combat loss rate is cxy, where c is the combat effectiveness coefficient of army Y in killing members of the guerilla army X.

The only way forces can gain members is through reinforcement. This gain can vary with circumstances on the battlefield. It is important to note that most of the short-term action in Lanchester's combat models is obtained through killing or operational deaths. Reinforcement thus becomes a crucial additional ingredient in any battlefield situation involving combat that extends over an appreciable length of time.

Scenario One

In the first scenario of Lanchester's combat models, two conventional armies are fighting. This scenario can be depicted as in Equations 4.7 and 4.8.

$$dx/dt = -ay - ex + f(t) \qquad [4.7]$$
$$dy/dt = -bx - ny + g(t) \qquad [4.8]$$

In Equations 4.7 and 4.8, parameter a is the combat effectiveness coefficient of army Y in killing army X, and parameter b is the comparable coefficient of army X in killing army Y. The operational loss rate for army X is determined by the term ex, and the comparable loss rate for army Y is determined by ny. All of these loss rates are preceded by negative signs, of course. The functions $f(t)$ and $g(t)$ are the reinforcement rates for armies X and Y, respectively.

This first scenario produces a linear system of two first-order interdependent ordinary differential equations. The behavioral characteristics of such a system can be highly varied, depending on the choice of parameter values. One way to approach the analysis of these equations is by manipulating their algebra directly. For example, one might naturally ask if there is an analytical method to discern from the algebra of the model how one army might have advantage over another, and indeed there is. If we say that there are no reinforcements, and that there are no operational loss rates, we can divide Equation 4.7 by Equation 4.8 to obtain $dx/dy = ay/bx$. We can integrate this using the separation of variables method to obtain

$$bx^2 = ay^2 + C,$$

where C is the constant of integration. Rearranging, this becomes $bx^2 - ay^2 = C$, which works for any solution to the differential equation system. This implies that army X will win the battle as long as $bx_0^2 > ay_0^2$. Here, x_0 and y_0 are the initial values of these variables. This is an example of Lanchester's "square law" as it applies to combat between conventional forces.

Scenario Two

The second scenario of Lanchester's combat models involves combat between one guerilla army and one conventional army. An interactive combat loss term is required only to describe losses to the guerilla army. This scenario can be described as in Equations 4.9 and 4.10.

$$dx/dt = -cxy - ex + f(t) \qquad [4.9]$$
$$dy/dt = -bx - ny + g(t) \qquad [4.10]$$

Note that the only algebraic difference between this scenario and that of Scenario One is the substitution of the term cxy for the combat loss rate for army X. This term makes this system of two differential equations nonlinear.

Scenario Three

The third scenario of Lanchester's combat models involves conflict between two guerilla armies. We can portray such a situation as in Equations 4.11 and 4.12.

$$dx/dt = -cxy - ex + f(t) \qquad [4.11]$$
$$dy/dt = -kxy - ny + g(t) \qquad [4.12]$$

In this instance, both armies have interactive combat loss rates.

Rapoport's Production and Exchange Model

The following model was developed by Anatol Rapoport (1960) and later adapted by Danby (1997, pp. 140–141). It is a useful example of the application of differential equations to be included here because it shows how such equations can be used in economics as well as social choice theory. The basic idea of the model is quite simple, although the analysis of the model reveals surprising complexities with respect to the behavior of individuals.

We begin with two individuals, X and Y. Both individuals produce goods, which we will identify respectively as x and y. To increase their happiness, each person desires to trade some of his or her own goods in order to obtain some of the goods that are produced by the other person. Working with proportions, if a person keeps p of her goods, then she trades q, where $q = 1 - p$. A person's happiness in having and trading goods is normally measured in terms of "utility," a term that is ubiquitous in economics and social choice discussions. Utility is used as a "common denominator" that allows the comparison of different things. For example, the goods produced by person X are presumably different from those produced by person Y. So it would be natural to ask how many units of x will be worth one unit of y in terms of a person's level of satisfaction or happiness. If one says that a person obtains so much utility from a unit of x, and so much utility from a unit of y, then we can simply add utilities to find out how much we get from having both x and y. We want to model change in the levels of x and y (i.e., changes in the level of goods produced by persons X and Y) as a consequence of their levels of utility.

To do this, we need to express the utility of persons X and Y in terms of gains and losses due to production and trade. Rapoport makes the assumption that people do not want to work unless they have to. Thus, there is a loss in utility due to having to produce goods. How much loss there is in utility is simply a function of how many goods are produced. But gains in utility are different. People like to have goods, so there is a gain in utility when they own the product of their labor as well as the product of another person's labor. Addressing an idea common to the subject of psychophysics known as Fechner's law (sometimes called Weber's law), individuals register arithmetic increases in perception only when the originating stimulus is increased geometrically. Thus, starting from a common base of zero dollars, a poor person will be greatly satisfied by a doubling of his or her goods, whereas a rich person will not receive the same level of satisfaction from a similar doubling. The original idea of Fechner's law is with respect to the perception of increases in physical stimuli such as light and sound from some base level.

Thus we can model each person's utility as

$$U_x = \log(1 + px + qy) - r_x x,$$
$$U_y = \log(1 + qx + py) - r_y y.$$

Here, U_i stands for person i's utility due to gains and losses in goods, the terms $-r_x x$ and $-r_y y$ represent losses in utility due to having to produce the goods, and the terms $\log(1 + px + qy)$ and $\log(1 + qx + py)$ are the gains in utility due to the possession of goods. The parameters for the loss terms are subscripted because it may be that person X feels differently about working for a living than person Y. The 1 in the log term is necessary to avoid negative values for gains when x and y are low [since $\log(1) = 0$].

But what we want to model is changes in x and y, not the utilities for persons X and Y. With the rational perspective embraced by this modeling concept, it is assumed that changes in the levels of production will only occur when there are changes in the level of utility. One approach to a specification is to express changes in x and y as proportional to the partial derivatives of their respective utility functions. Thus, we can state that

$$\frac{dx}{dt} = c_x\left(\frac{p}{(1 + px + qy)} - r_x\right),$$ [4.13]

$$\frac{dy}{dt} = c_y\left(\frac{p}{(1 + qx + py)} - r_y\right).$$ [4.14]

The analysis of this model begins with determining the equilibrium values. Numerical investigations of this model then begin by assuming various values of the parameters. Sometimes this is done by setting $c_x = c_y$ and $r_x = r_y$. Phase diagrams can be constructed that portray various behaviors of this model given the changes in the parameter values. For example, parasitism occurs when either X or Y (but not both) stops producing goods, a consequence of a long term and serious overall trade imbalance that can result from even slight relative differences in a work ethic (i.e., parameters r_x and r_y). This fascinating model can be easily extended to portray interactions between nations, not just individual people.

Summary

This chapter presents three classic examples of differential equation modeling from the social sciences. All three of these examples involve systems of first-order differential equations. The first two models, Richardson's arms race model and Lanchester's combat model, address military concepts. They are among the most widely referenced models with social science themes in the entire literature of differential equation modeling. Both models have algebraic components that were previously found in the predator-prey model discussed in the previous chapter. The final social science model introduced in this chapter is Rapoport's production and exchange model, a model with an economic theme. This is an example with a more complex algebraic structure, and it helps show how differential equation modeling may be used to address issues such as consumer preference and/or individual utility. These examples, as interesting as they are, only begin to touch the breadth and potential for differential equation modeling in the social sciences. More advanced models that push the boundaries of model specification in new and interesting ways are increasingly appearing in social scientific research.

5. TRANSFORMING SECOND-ORDER AND NONAUTONOMOUS DIFFERENTIAL EQUATIONS INTO SYSTEMS OF FIRST-ORDER DIFFERENTIAL EQUATIONS

So far in this book, we have discussed only first-order differential equations. However, sometimes a theorist needs to work with a model that involves a derivative of a higher order, such as a second-order derivative. Indeed, we have already been working with second-order derivatives indirectly since systems of first-order differential equations can be expressed in terms of second-order differential equations, as was discussed in relation to Richardson's arms race model in the previous chapter. In general, we rarely need to worry about transforming a system of first-order differential equations into a second-order differential equation since all of the techniques presented in this book work with first-order systems. A problem occurs, however, when we start out with a second-order differential equation and need to transform it into a system of first-order equations to conduct our analyses using these same techniques.

In the physical sciences it is quite common to encounter second-order differential equation models. Again, Newton's law relating force to the product of mass and acceleration is a second-order differential equation since acceleration is the derivative of velocity, which itself is a derivative. But in the social sciences, most differential equation models start out as first-order systems. Why then might it be important for social scientists to know how to transform second-order differential equations into first-order systems if they are going to be working with first-order systems in the first place? There are two answers to this, one technical and the other substantive. The first is that all modelers learn from the examples of others, and large numbers of second-order differential equation models exist that exhibit extraordinary properties that social scientists will want to study. For example, the program Phaser comes with a large inventory of dynamical systems that may be understood in terms of second-order differential equations. Unless we can examine and understand the works of others, how can we proceed with our own innovations? But the second answer to the above question is that similar mathematical models can often approximate dynamical processes that originate from very different fields of study. Thus, it is likely that social scientists will encounter second-order differential equation models originating in the physical and natural sciences that are isomorphic in structure to models that they might want to apply with respect to social and political phenomena that have similar dynamical properties. This is a point argued eloquently by Anatol Rapoport, a mathematician with an expansive view of mathematical modeling across many fields (Rapoport, 1983, pp. 25–26).

Again, second-order differential equations are those in which a second derivative exists (as the highest order) in the equation. For example, Equation 5.1 is a homogeneous and linear differential equation with constant coefficients.

$$a\frac{d^2y}{dt^2} + b\frac{dy}{dt} + cy = 0 \qquad [5.1]$$

Equation 5.1 is homogeneous because the right-hand side is set equal to zero. It is linear because there are no nonlinear elements in the equation, such as y^2. It has constant coefficients because the parameters a, b, and c do not vary. If the right-hand side of Equation 5.1 is not equal to zero, then the equation is nonhomogeneous.

There are two general approaches to working with second-order linear differential equations. The first is to find explicit solutions for such equations, while the second involves rephrasing the problem in terms of a system of first-order equations. In terms of finding explicit solutions for second-order linear differential equations, this is a bit of an art form since it can involve some intelligent guessing (often called a "guess and test" method), followed by rules for exploiting the initial guesses to obtain a complete and general solution for the equation. In this chapter, I discuss an alternative approach to working with second- and higher-order differential equations that reframes the problem in terms of systems of first-order differential equations.

There are a variety of reasons for emphasizing this alternative approach here. First, the methods that are appropriate for finding general solutions to second- and higher-order linear differential equations are less useful for nonlinear differential equations. Second, detailed discussions of such approaches with regard to second- and higher-order linear differential equations are quite standard, and they can easily be found in any number of other books on differential equations. Also, I cover much of this material in the next chapter in a discussion related to stability analyses for differential equation systems. Interested readers can find useful and complete discussions of approaches to finding explicit solutions to second- and higher-order linear differential equations in Blanchard et al. (2006, see especially pp. 324–329), as well as Zill (2005, Chap. 4).

More important, the alternative methods mentioned above can be used to resolve the qualitative behavior of second- and higher-order linear differential equations in a manner that finds correspondence with the overall approach to differential equation modeling that is used throughout this book. Indeed, these other methods are preferable for our purposes since they rephrase the issue of explicit solutions for second- and higher-order differential equations to one involving systems of first-order differential equations. It is necessary to do this if one wants to use numerical analyses to study differential equations, and, indeed, this approach is increasingly favored by many mathematicians. Nonetheless, readers should note that the approach preferred here (working with systems of first-order differential equations) is by no means the approach favored by all, and some readers may find traditional approaches to finding explicit solutions to second- and higher-order linear differential equations to be helpful in some situations. The discussion of this subject in the next chapter within the context of stability analyses will be useful in this regard.

Second- and Higher-Order
Differential Equations

It is easy to transform a second- and higher-order differential equation into a system of first-order differential equations (e.g., see Blanchard et al., 2005, pp. 159–161). There is no loss of information or generality in doing this. Again, this type of transformation is necessary to study second- or higher-order differential equations using numerical methods.

Let us say that we have a differential equation that is of any order higher than first-order. To transform this equation into a system of first-order differential equations, begin by isolating the highest-order derivative on one side, putting everything else on the other. For example, let us begin with Equation 5.2, using notation and phrasing suggested by Koçak (1989, pp. 6–7).

$$\frac{d^n y}{dt^n} = F\left(y, \frac{dy}{dt}, \dots, \frac{d^{n-1}y}{dt^{n-1}}\right) \qquad [5.2]$$

To proceed, we will need initial conditions for everything except the highest derivative (i.e., the left-hand side in Equation 5.2). Thus, we require the initial conditions

$$y(t_0), dy/dt \text{ at } t_0, \text{ all the way up to } d^{n-1}y/dt^{n-1} \text{ at } t_0. \qquad [5.3]$$

Now we need to introduce new variables. These variables will take the place of y, dy/dt, and all other derivatives up to $d^{n-1}y/dt^{n-1}$. Since all of these things vary, we are making variables out of all of them, and considering them as separate dimensions in a system of equations. The new variables look like this:

$$x_1(t) = y,$$
$$x_2(t) = dy/dt, \ldots,$$
$$x_n(t) = d^{n-1}y/dt^{n-1}. \qquad [5.4]$$

Now we want to take the derivatives of all of the x_i new variables so that we can establish our system of differential equations using those derivatives. Thus we have

$dx_1/dt = x_2$, (from Equation 5.4)

$dx_2/dt = x_3$, (again, from Equation 5.4)

$dx_n/dt = F(x_1, x_2, \ldots, x_n)$, (from Equation 5.2 after substituting x_i).

We can use an RK4 method with this set of equations in the normal manner. Remember that we will need the initial conditions for these variables, which we obtain from Equation 5.3. Thus,

$$x_1(t_0) = y(t_0),$$
$$x_2(t_0) = dy/dt(t_0), \ldots,$$
$$x_n(t_0) = d^{n-1}y/dt^{n-1}(t_0),$$

and we are finished.

An Example

Consider the second-order differential Equation 5.5,

$$\frac{d^2y}{dt^2} = -7\frac{dy}{dt} - 10y. \qquad [5.5]$$

We begin by setting up our new variables, x_i. Thus we have,

$$x_1(t) = y, \text{ and } x_2(t) = dy/dt, \qquad [5.6]$$

and our new set of first-order differential equations is found using substitution:

$$dx_1/dt = x_2,$$
$$dx_2/dt = -7x_2 - 10x_1.$$

We need only initial conditions for y (which is x_1) and dy/dt (which is x_2) in order to conduct a numerical analysis using an RK4 method with this system. Other helpful examples can be found in Koçak (1989, pp. 6–7).

Nonautonomous Differential Equations

In politics, an "autonomous" region or body is self-governing. One can even have an autonomous committee in, say, a university. The idea is that the region or body does not depend on external conditions for its operations. For example, a truly autonomous body does not have to ask for permission to do something. With differential equations, the meaning is quite similar. Autonomous differential equations operate based on their own internal values. In practical terms, this means that an autonomous system of differential equations operates based only on the values of its dependent variables. But a nonautonomous system requires information other than from its dependent variables. It requires the value of the independent variable as well. Thus, nonautonomous differential equations are those in which the independent variable t is explicitly included in the model. For example, Equation 5.7 is a nonautonomous differential equation containing what is called a "forced oscillator" component.

$$dx/dt = ay - mx + g[\cos(pt)] \qquad [5.7]$$

Readers will note that this equation is a modification of Equation 4.1 for Richardson's arms race model. Here, the assumption is made that country X will experience cyclical variations in its concern regarding its armament spending. These variations could be a consequence of, say, an electoral cycle in which the leaders of the country try to whip up fear of country Y right before regularly scheduled elections in an effort to gain fear-based votes. Since the value of the independent variable t is included explicitly in the model, the model is not self-governing.

There are a few ways to handle the inclusion of the independent variable in the model when conducting numerical experiments. One way is simply to keep track of the value of t as one proceeds forward in time according to the step size for the RK4 method. But a more general (yet equivalent) approach is to increase the dimension of the system by one by creating a new equation that does this for you. Thus, you establish a new variable, x_{n+1}, where n is the number of dimensions (i.e., dependent variables) in the original differential equation system. The new differential equation is

$$\frac{dx_{n+1}}{dt} = 1, \qquad [5.8]$$

with an initial condition of $x_{n+1}(0) = t_0$.

Integrating Equation 5.8 with respect to t produces the solution $x_{n+1} = t + t_0$ (see also Koçak, 1989, pp. 7 and 8). Now that we have this new variable, x_{n+1}, we can substitute it for t wherever it occurs in our system.

For example, our new version of Richardson's arms race model using this approach would be

$$dx_1/dt = ax_2 - mx_1 + g[\cos(px_3)], \qquad [5.9]$$

$$dx_2/dt = bx_1 - nx_2 + h, \qquad [5.10]$$

$$dx_3/dt = 1, \text{with } x_3(0) = t_0. \qquad [5.11]$$

Note that I have changed the variables to be of the form x_i. It is interesting to note that this version of Richardson's arms race model has the potential to encounter high degrees of longitudinal variability due to the inclusion of a forced oscillator term in Equation 5.9 (see Brown, 1995b).

Summary

This chapter initially focuses on methods to transform a second- or higher-order differential equation into a system of first-order differential equations. One of the main purposes of doing this is to allow one to experiment numerically with second- or higher-order models that are abundant in the natural and physical sciences. The numerical methods presented in this book (such as the RK4) only work with first-order systems, so transforming higher-order equations into first-order systems is a necessity in this regard. It is not uncommon for a social scientist to find dynamic parallels between a social process and, say, one or more aspects of a physical process that is modeled by a second-order differential equation. Having the flexibility to work with higher-order models in this manner gives a theorist the intellectual power to exploit the higher-order dynamics that are associated with such models.

Similarly, this chapter then presents a method for working with nonautonomous differential equations. The approach is comparable with that used for higher-order differential equations, in the sense that one increases the dimension of the system (in this case by one) as a means of keeping track of the independent variable t. Thus, a single nonautonomous differential equation can be rewritten as a system of two first-order autonomous differential equations. The numerical methods used in this book (such as the RK4) can then work with this system in the standard manner as with all first-order systems.

6. STABILITY ANALYSES OF LINEAR DIFFERENTIAL EQUATION SYSTEMS

The analysis of differential equation models nearly always involves a minimum of three primary aspects. The first is to identify the equilibrium points and their basins of attraction for the system. This may or may not include the identification of equilibrium marshes. The second is to describe the behavior of trajectories for the dependent variables within the overall relevant phase space. And the third is to characterize the behavior of trajectories that pass within close proximity of the equilibrium points. The current chapter focuses on this third aspect with respect to systems of first-order linear differential equations.

Systems of differential equations usually behave similarly (with occasional exceptions) within the neighborhood of an equilibrium point regardless of whether or not the equations are linear or nonlinear. Further away from the equilibrium points, the behaviors of linear and nonlinear differential equations may differ markedly, and the numerical techniques presented earlier in this book are of great importance in describing these behaviors. But near an equilibrium point in two-dimensional systems, there are six fundamental behaviors, and it is important to be able to recognize each one. We can identify these behaviors clearly by examining the linear case.

A Motivating Example of How Stability Can Dramatically Change in One System

First let us motivate this discussion of stability analysis by showing how easy it is for a differential equation system to have equilibria that may exhibit wildly different stability characteristics depending on the values of the system parameters. Let us reconsider Richardson's arms race model. Recall from Equations 4.3 and 4.4 that the equilibrium values for Richardson's arms race model are given as $X^* = (ah + gn)/(mn - ab)$ and $Y^* = (bg - hm)/(mn - ab)$. As mentioned previously, this equilibrium exists so long as $mn - ab \neq 0$. It is possible to vary the parameters such that the equilibrium point (X^*, Y^*) remains approximately the same despite the fact that the parameters are changing. This would require changing more than one parameter value at a time such that the equilibrium solution remains the same. In the real world, an observer of this system might not detect any difference since the observer would observe only, say, the steady level of arms purchases for each nation as characterized by a stable equilibrium point. But if the parameters change such that the quantity $mn - ab$ alternates from a positive value to a negative one (i.e., $mn < ab$), then the stability of the equilibrium value suddenly changes from being stable to unstable (see Richardson, 1960, pp. 24–28, as well as Rapoport, 1983, pp. 126–128). Substantively, this means, for example, that one can suddenly find oneself in a runaway arms race when recent history suggested everything was "safe" and stable. In the words of the comic, you never saw it coming.

The phenomenon described above is related to a field of dynamical modeling called "catastrophe theory," a subject I have written about and applied empirically elsewhere (Brown, 1995a, 1995b). This addresses the idea that the behavioral dynamics of macro social systems are dependent on the local stability characteristics of certain states or system equilibria. Some scientists have dealt with sudden change by establishing thresholds for their systems. When certain parameter values pass beyond those thresholds, then the system's behavior can change, as if there are two sets of "laws" governing the system, each one applicable for different situations. However, Rapoport has argued that this is ad hoc, in the sense that it describes the behavior of the system without describing its underlying structure (Rapoport, 1983, p. 127). When catastrophe theory is applied to differential equations, one can describe the sudden behavioral change of a system by directly relying on its underlying mechanisms.

This should help motivate the study of differential equation system stability. Understanding what causes a system to be stable or unstable, or to have a certain kind of stability or instability, brings us into a new world of possibilities for understanding social systems. Indeed, this is currently an exciting area of research in the application of differential equation systems to real-world phenomena.

Scalar Methods

To describe the six fundamental behaviors of two-dimensional differential equation systems near an equilibrium point, let us work with the system of linear differential equations presented here as Equations 6.1 and 6.2. These equations are nearly identical to Richardson's arms race model.

$$dx/dt = ax + by \qquad [6.1]$$
$$dy/dt = cx + ky \qquad [6.2]$$

First, let us note that the origin is the equilibrium for this system, which can be obtained either by inspection or by setting both Equations 6.1 and 6.2 equal to zero, and then solving the two simultaneous equations. Now let us rephrase Equations 6.1 and 6.2 as one higher-order differential equation by first differentiating Equation 6.1. Thus, we have

$$\frac{d^2x}{dt^2} = a\frac{dx}{dt} + b\frac{dy}{dt}. \qquad [6.3]$$

The next step is to substitute dy/dt from Equation 6.2 and y from Equation 6.1 into 6.3 to obtain Equation 6.4.

$$\frac{d^2x}{dt^2} - (a+k)\frac{dx}{dt} + (ak - bc)x = 0 \qquad [6.4]$$

This is a second-order differential equation which we will solve using the "guess and test method" (see Blanchard et al., 2005, pp. 117–120, 194–195).

Let us make a guess and say that $x = Ae^{rt}$, which introduces the constant parameter r and the arbitrary constant A, and we are hoping that this may offer a solution for x. Again, a solution for x would be an algebraic function that does not have any derivatives in it that would give us values of x for any given value of the independent variable, t. The possible solution Ae^{rt} is a "thoughtful" guess inspired by the solution for the related first-order linear differential equation (see Equation 2.4) and the idea that if the linear combination of the various derivatives in Equation 6.4 all cancel out to equal zero, then the derivatives would probably be repetitious in some manner.

Note that $dx/dt = rAe^{rt}$ and $d^2x/dt^2 = r^2Ae^{rt}$. Let us substitute these values into Equation 6.4 to obtain Equation 6.5.

$$r^2Ae^{rt} - (a+k)rAe^{rt} + (ak - bc)Ae^{rt} = 0 \qquad [6.5]$$

Factoring out the term Ae^{rt} and noting that $e^{rt} \neq 0$, we extract what is called the "characteristic equation," shown here as Equation 6.6.

$$r^2 - (a+k)r + (ak - bc) = 0 \qquad [6.6]$$

Thus, it seems that our possible solution, $x = Ae^{rt}$, can work as long as we can find appropriate values of the parameter r.

We are concerned about the behavior of the system of two differential equations (6.1 and 6.2) in the neighborhood of the equilibrium (0, 0). Our solution for our dependent variables depends on the values of the roots for the characteristic equation, which we can solve using the quadratic formula, or with higher-order systems, Newton's method. In the case of x, we want to find values for the parameter r for which Equation 6.6 is true given the values of the other parameters ($a, b, c,$ and k). Note that there will be two roots (r_1 and r_2) for Equation 6.6. If we tried simply to use $x = Ae^{rt}$ as our solution, we would have two different solutions for x. But what we want is one general solution for x, not two separate solutions. Thus, we need to find a way to combine the two solutions into one solution.

In the theory of differential equations, there is something called the principle of superposition (Zill, 2005, pp. 130–134). This principle is also called the linearity principle (see Blanchard et al., 2005, pp. 114–116; also Morris and Brown, 1952, pp. 69–71). The essence of this principle has two parts. The first is that if one finds one solution to a differential equation, then if you multiply that solution by a constant, the result is also a solution to the differential equation. This part can be easily verified. Since we have Ae^{rt} as one solution for x, try substituting sAe^{rt} (and its derivatives) into Equation 6.4 as was done previously to obtain Equation 6.5. You will see that the parameter s will divide out and be eliminated, leaving us again with Equation 6.5.

The second part of the principle of superposition states that if you have two solutions for your differential equation, then any linear combination of those two solutions is also a solution to the differential equation. This can easily be extended to equations of higher order (i.e., with more solutions placed in a linear combination). This linear combination of the two solutions is the general solution to the homogeneous second-order differential equation, and we will see how this is done below.

Keep in mind that we are doing all of this so that we can determine the behavior of the dependent variables for our system of differential equations. We now know that our solutions for our second-order differential equations will involve a parameter r, for which there will be two values (i.e., roots). This means that the behavior of our differential equation will depend on the roots of the characteristic Equation 6.6.

At this point it is useful for us to work with real numbers to show how this works. In this instance, I will employ parameter values suggested by Danby (1997, pp. 52–54). Let us specify an example system of the form found in Equations 6.1 and 6.2, which is shown here as Equations 6.7 and 6.8.

$$dx/dt = 2x + y \qquad [6.7]$$
$$dy/dt = x + 2y \qquad [6.8]$$

This means that $a = 2, b = 1, c = 1$, and $k = 2$. Substituting these parameter values into Equation 6.6, we have Equation 6.9.

$$r^2 - 4r + 3 = 0 \qquad [6.9]$$

Using the quadratic formula, we find that $r_1 = 1$ and $r_2 = 3$.

Now we need to use these roots to arrive at a general solution for our system. Since our system is interdependent, and thus x depends on y and vice versa, we are going to need solutions for both x and y. We shall use our guessing method, and say that $x = Ae^{rt}$ and $y = Be^{rt}$. A nice approach is to note that $dx/dt = rAe^{rt}$ and $dy/dt = rBe^{rt}$, and then to substitute these values into our original differential equations, 6.7 and 6.8. Doing this yields

$$rAe^{rt} = 2(Ae^{rt}) + Be^{rt},$$
$$rBe^{rt} = Ae^{rt} + 2(Be^{rt}).$$

Dividing through both equations by e^{rt} and then rearranging yields the equivalent expressions,

$$A(2 - r) + B = 0,$$
$$A + B(2 - r) = 0.$$

Note that these two equations will produce nontrivial solutions for A and B (Hadley, 1961, p. 174) only if

$$\det\begin{pmatrix} 2 - r & 1 \\ 1 & 2 - r \end{pmatrix} = 0.$$

This is another way of getting the characteristic equation of the system, and I include it here so that readers can note an important similarity between the scalar methods used here and the matrix methods described further below. Solving for this gives us our roots, $r_1 = 1$ and $r_2 = 3$, as before. But now let us take these roots and use them to solve for A and B using the above two simultaneous equations. Note that when $r_1 = 1$, then $A = -B$, and when $r_2 = 3$, then $A = B$, with A being arbitrary in each instance, allowing us to rewrite and consolidate our terms with an A_1 and an A_2.

Now we can write our solutions in terms of only A_i. Thus we have four solutions of interest. They are

$$x = A_1 e^t,$$
$$y = -A_1 e^t,$$

and

$$x = A_2 e^{3t},$$
$$y = A_2 e^{3t}.$$

Due to the principle of superposition, our general solution should be a linear combination of two solutions. This means that our general solutions for the second-order differential equation as expressed in Equation 6.4 for variable x, as well as the comparable version for y, are

$$x = A_1 e^t + A_2 e^{3t}, \qquad [6.10]$$
$$y = -A_1 e^t + A_2 e^{3t}, \qquad [6.11]$$

where A_i are arbitrary constants that depend on initial conditions for x and y. These constants are similar in nature to the constant y_0 found in Equation 2.4 with respect to a first-order linear difference equation. Note that Equations 6.10 and 6.11 are linear combinations of two separate solutions for x and y, each of which uses one of the two roots for Equation 6.9.

At this point it should be clear that the behavior of our dependent variables, x and y, over time will depend qualitatively on the values of the roots of the characteristic equation. Inspection of Equations 6.10 and 6.11 reveals that as time increases, the magnitudes of x and y will increase exponentially since both of the roots (in this case, real numbers) are positive. This means that our equilibrium value for this system as defined by Equations 6.7 and 6.8 is unstable, and the equilibrium value itself (i.e., the origin) is called an "unstable node."

Matrix Methods

At this point we need to step back and examine a different approach utilizing matrices to evaluate the qualitative behavior of a linear system of differential equations. In my view, this matrix approach is both more general and preferable (for reasons that I explain below), although some readers may continue to favor the guess and test method of finding solutions as described above. This matrix approach works with linear differential equations, but it can also be expanded conceptually to work with nonlinear differential equations, as I explain in the next chapter.

We begin by restating the system of two differential equations (6.1 and 6.2) in matrix form. We do not collapse the system into one second-order equation as was done previously. Thus, in matrix form, we write our original equations as

$$dY/dt = AY, \qquad [6.12]$$

where

$$A = \begin{pmatrix} 2 & 1 \\ 1 & 2 \end{pmatrix},$$

and the elements of matrix A (called the "coefficient matrix") are the coefficients of our system of Equations 6.7 and 6.8. The vector Y has two elements, x and y, which are the dependent variables of our system. More generally, in terms of Equations 6.1 and 6.2,

$$\frac{dY}{dt} = \begin{pmatrix} dx/dt \\ dy/dt \end{pmatrix} = \begin{pmatrix} ax + by \\ cx + ky \end{pmatrix} = \begin{pmatrix} a & b \\ c & k \end{pmatrix} \begin{pmatrix} x \\ y \end{pmatrix}. \qquad [6.13]$$

From the principle of superposition, we know that we can manufacture a solution to this system of equations by linearly combining any two given solutions. Thus, if $Y_1(t)$ and $Y_2(t)$ are solutions to the system (Equation 6.13), then we can say that

$$w_1 Y_1(t) + w_2 Y_2(t) \qquad [6.14]$$

is also a solution to the system. Here, we are using w_i to represent arbitrary constants. Since we need two solutions in order to do this, we obtain them by looking for two special solutions for which a scalar can have the same effect on vector **Y** as the original coefficient matrix when we multiply the two together. (In many instances, these solutions can be called "straight-line solutions" since they can identify trajectories in a phase diagram that are straight lines. See Blanchard et al., 2006, pp. 258–271.) Thus, we are really looking for two things. We need a scalar that acts the same as the coefficient matrix, but we also need the values of our dependent variables that will cooperate with this scalar such that it produces the same result as the coefficient matrix when they are multiplied together as in Equation 6.13.

Let us group these desired values of the dependent variable in the vector **V**. Thus, **V** = (x, y), and we are looking for values of **V** such that

$$\mathbf{AV} = \mathbf{A}\begin{pmatrix} x \\ y \end{pmatrix} = \lambda \begin{pmatrix} x \\ y \end{pmatrix} = \lambda \mathbf{V} \qquad [6.15]$$

or alternatively, $(\mathbf{A} - \lambda\mathbf{I})\mathbf{V} = 0$. Here, λ is the scalar that acts the same as the coefficient matrix, **A**, when multiplied by the vector **V**, and **I** is the identity matrix. The scalar λ is called an "eigenvalue" of **A**, and the vector **V** is called the "eigenvector" that corresponds to the eigenvalue λ. Another way of writing Equation 6.15 in component form is

$$ax + by = \lambda x,$$
$$cx + ky = \lambda y,$$

or equivalently,

$$(a - \lambda)x + by = 0, \qquad [6.16]$$
$$cx + (k - \lambda)y = 0. \qquad [6.17]$$

Nontrivial solutions for this system exist only if **det** $|\mathbf{A} - \lambda\mathbf{I}| = 0$. Thus, in component form, we evaluate

$$\mathbf{det}\begin{pmatrix} a - \lambda & b \\ c & k - \lambda \end{pmatrix} = 0. \qquad [6.18]$$

Equation 6.18 involves the algebraic expansion

$$\lambda^2 - (a + k)\lambda + (ak - bc) = 0,$$

which is the system's "characteristic polynomial." The eigenvalues of the coefficient matrix, **A**, are the roots of this polynomial. Since this is a quadratic equation, there are two roots. Using the example from our linear system (Equation 6.12), we can rewrite Equation 6.18 as

$$\det \begin{pmatrix} 2 - \lambda & 1 \\ 1 & 2 - \lambda \end{pmatrix} = 0$$

or, after expansion, $\lambda^2 - 4\lambda + 3 = 0$. Here, $\lambda_1 = 1$, and $\lambda_2 = 3$.

Note that our eigenvalues for the coefficient matrix are identical to the roots of the characteristic equation as found from Equation 6.9 using scalar methods. This is not an accident. Indeed, we will soon see that we have been working with eigenvalues all along when we calculated the roots to the characteristic Equation 6.6 and that even our parameter a in Equation 2.4 is an eigenvalue of a simple one-dimensional first-order linear differential equation.

Now that we have the eigenvalues for the system (Equation 6.12), we need to obtain our eigenvectors. There will be two eigenvectors, one for each eigenvalue. We obtain the eigenvectors by substituting the eigenvalues (one at a time) into $(\mathbf{A} - \lambda\mathbf{I})\mathbf{V} = 0$, having obtained this expression from Equation 6.15. This is equivalent to solving simultaneously the scalar forms of the Equations 6.16 and 6.17. Continuing in matrix form for our example, we obtain our eigenvector corresponding to eigenvalue $\lambda_1 = 1$ by solving the system

$$\begin{pmatrix} 2 - \lambda & 1 \\ 1 & 2 - \lambda \end{pmatrix} \mathbf{V} = \begin{pmatrix} 1 & 1 \\ 1 & 1 \end{pmatrix} \begin{pmatrix} x \\ y \end{pmatrix} = 0. \qquad [6.19]$$

In component form, this yields two redundant equations, both of which are $x + y = 0$. This means that $x = -y$, and any vector of the form $(-y, y)$ is an eigenvector associated with $\lambda_1 = 1$, as long as $y \neq 0$. For example, $(-1, 1)$, $(2, -2)$, and $(-5, 5)$ are all equivalent eigenvectors associated with the eigenvalue $\lambda_1 = 1$. We will identify this eigenvector as $\mathbf{V}_1 = (-y, y)$.

For the case in which $\lambda_2 = 3$, we solve the system again and obtain component equations

$$(2 - 3)x + 1y = 0,$$
$$1x + (2 - 3)y = 0.$$

This yields two redundant equations, both of which are $x = y$. This means that any vector of the form (y, y) is an eigenvector for this system that is associated with the eigenvalue $\lambda_2 = 3$, and $(1, 1)$ would be an example of such an eigenvector. We will identify this eigenvector as $\mathbf{V}_2 = (y, y)$.

Some readers will note that $\mathbf{V}_1$ and $\mathbf{V}_2$ are linearly independent and thus constitute a basis for $\mathbb{R}^2$. This means that any linear combination of these vectors will allow us to arrive at any given point in $\mathbb{R}^2$. Using this fact in combination with Equation 6.13, we can now write the general solution for this differential equation system as

$$Y(t) = w_1 e^{1t} \mathbf{V}_1 + w_2 e^{3t} \mathbf{V}_2. \qquad [6.20]$$

Keep in mind that each vector $\mathbf{V}_1$ and $\mathbf{V}_2$ has both x and y components. It does not matter which eigenvector we use in our solution as long as it is in the appropriate form. For example, since $(-1, 1)$, $(1, -1)$, and $(2, -2)$ are all examples of eigenvectors associated with $\lambda_1 = 1$ (because they are all scalar multiples of one another), we can use any one of them in a solution. For simplicity, I will use eigenvector $(1, -1)$ to be associated with $\lambda_1 = 1$, and eigenvector $(1, 1)$ to be associated with $\lambda_2 = 3$. In terms of our example, this means that our x coordinate for any solution to our differential equation system [call it $x(t)$] will be $x(t) = w_1 e^t + w_2 e^{3t}$, and the y coordinate for our system [call it $y(t)$] will be $y(t) = -w_1 e^t + w_2 e^{3t}$. This is the same as we obtained previously using scalar methods. (See Equations 6.10 and 6.11.) The only thing left to do is to solve for the arbitrary constants, w_1 and w_2, and for this we set $t = 0$ and use the initial conditions for our dependent variables, x_0 and y_0, to solve the two simultaneous equations.

To sum up, we want to state that the general solution form for our system of two first-order linear differential equations with two real, unequal, and positive eigenvalues (λ_j) is given as Equation 6.21.

$$Y(t) = w_1 e^{\lambda_1 t} \mathbf{V}_1 + w_2 e^{\lambda_2 t} \mathbf{V}_2 \qquad [6.21]$$

Here, $\mathbf{V}_j$ are the eigenvectors, and w_j are the arbitrary constants that depend on the initial conditions of the dependent variables.

There are now two important points to make. First, the procedures for obtaining general solutions for first-order differential equation systems as outlined above are somewhat different for situations in which the eigenvalues are repeated (i.e., both have the same value), there exists a zero eigenvalue, or the eigenvalues are complex [involving the imaginary number $i (i = \sqrt{-1})$]. In a way, that is the bad news, since we would need to know those other methods in order to come up with general solutions to other linear systems. But the second point is equally valuable, and it is the good news. *The qualitative behavior of the dependent variables over time for a system of first-order linear differential equations depends on the eigenvalues of the system, not the eigenvectors or the arbitrary constants.* This can be seen through inspection of Equation 6.21, a point that is also demonstrated through example below. Moreover, since the approach recommended in this book is to use numerical techniques to solve and plot systems of ordinary first-order differential equations, once we understand the importance of the eigenvalues for linear systems, we do not need to find the general explicit solutions to the equations. All we really need are the eigenvalues themselves. It is worth pointing out, of course, that the general solutions of linear systems were more important to the practical application of systems of linear differential equations before the arrival of fast computers capable of doing the number of calculations necessary for numerical analysis.

Equilibrium Categories

Why then did I have you (the reader) go through all the above steps to obtain a general solution to a system of linear differential equations? It is necessary to do this at least once in order to understand the dominant importance of the eigenvalues. Once one understands that neither the arbitrary constants nor the eigenvectors affect the qualitative behavior of the linear differential equation systems, we can dispense with finding the eigenvectors and arbitrary constants entirely. Rather, we can move freely into classifying the behavior of linear systems according to their eigenvalues only, and then we can move directly to the use of numerical methods to solve for the differential equations. It is difficult to overstate the importance of this point.

While the equilibrium categories described below are applicable to linear two-dimensional differential equation systems, they are not adequate for nonlinear higher-dimensional systems. For example, nonlinear systems with three or higher dimensions can potentially have a "strange attractor," which is a phenomenon associated with chaos theory (Brown, 1995b). Chaos can also appear in nonautonomous nonlinear systems of two dimensions. Nonetheless, the list below is a necessary beginning to the study of all differential equation systems regardless of order and linearity. This is emphasized further in the next chapter with respect to nonlinear differential equation systems.

Unstable Nodes

Let us now pull all this together by categorizing various types of behaviors that autonomous first-order linear differential equation systems of two dimensions can have near an equilibrium point. We begin with our first example as defined by the parameter values found in Equations 6.7 and 6.8. Here the eigenvalues are $\lambda_i = (1, 3)$, positive, real, and unequal. From

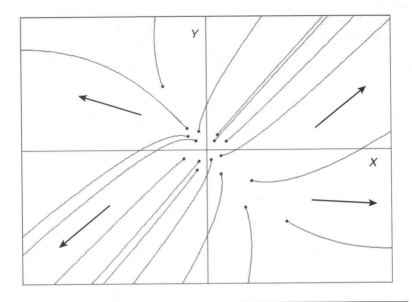

Figure 6.1 A Two-Dimensional Linear Model With an Unstable Node

NOTE: The initial conditions are represented as dots. All movement extends away from the initial conditions along the trajectories shown.

either Equations 6.10 and 6.11 or Equation 6.20 we can see that the dependent variables will continue to increase without bound as time increases. This produces an unstable node at the origin, which is the equilibrium point for this system. This type of equilibrium point is called a "source." The meaning of the term is drawn from the idea that trajectories move away from this point just as light from the sun moves outward and away from the sun. A phase diagram for this system (using Phaser) is shown here in Figure 6.1. Note that all trajectories move away from the origin. This is the characteristic of an unstable equilibrium point.

Stable Nodes

If we change the parameter values of the system so that $a = -4$, $b = 1$, $c = 1$, and $k = -2$, then the behavior of trajectories near the origin differs dramatically from that shown in Figure 6.1. Now the eigenvalues are $\lambda_i = -3 \pm \sqrt{2}$, negative, real, and unequal. Inspection of Equation 6.21 shows that the term $e^{\lambda_i t}$ decays to zero over time in the presence of negative eigenvalues. With these new parameters, the trajectories move inward toward the equilibrium. In this setting, the origin is now a "stable node."

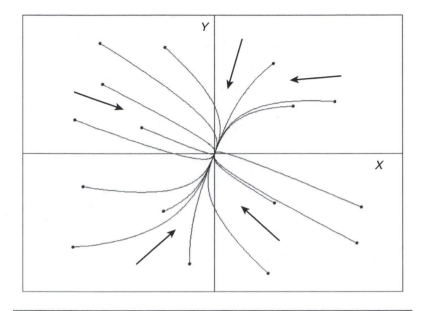

Figure 6.2   A Two-Dimensional Linear Model With a Stable Node

NOTE: The initial conditions are represented as dots. All movement extends away from the initial conditions along the trajectories shown, converging at the node in the center of the plot.

This type of equilibrium is also called a "sink." The phase diagram of this system is shown in Figure 6.2. Note in this figure that all of the trajectories move toward the origin, and this type of behavior is the characteristic of a stable equilibrium acting within its basin of attraction.

Saddle Points

If we change the parameter values of our linear system again to be $a = 1$, $b = 4$, $c = 2$, and $k = -1$, the eigenvalues now become $\lambda_i = (3, -3)$. Here, one root is real and positive while the other is real and negative. As one might expect, this situation creates what is in essence a merger between a sink and a source. The equilibrium point is now called a "saddle point." The term is made to reflect the nature of a horse's saddle. From two opposite directions, the equilibrium point acts as a sink, with nearby trajectories being pulled toward the origin. From a different set of two opposite directions, the equilibrium point acts as a source, with nearby trajectories being pulled away from the origin. Only one straight-line solution actually gets

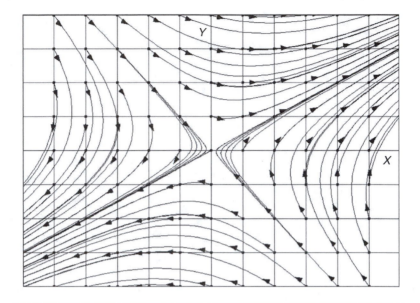

Figure 6.3   A Two-Dimensional Linear Model: The Origin as a Saddle Point

permanently pulled toward the origin, however. All other trajectories eventually become influenced by the outward pull and turn to move away from the equilibrium. Such an equilibrium point is unstable.

This is a more complicated situation than a simple source or sink. Figure 6.3 portrays the phase portrait for this system in the neighborhood of the origin. A direction field is added to the diagram to assist in showing the direction of movement for the trajectories. The starting points for all trajectory flows are marked with a dot. Note that trajectories that begin near the top left or the bottom right of the diagram get initially pulled toward the origin. But eventually the unstable characteristics of the positive eigenvalue dominate the system and the trajectories move away from the origin in either the first or third quadrants. It is this unbounded behavior that makes a saddle point unstable.

Unstable Spirals

When we change the parameter values of the system to be $a = 1$, $b = 4$, $c = -2$, and $k = 1$, the eigenvalues become complex with both real and imaginary parts. Here, $\lambda_i = 1 \pm i\sqrt{8}$. This situation produces trajectories that are unstable spirals. The spirals result from the imaginary components

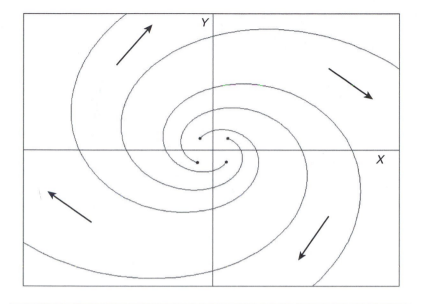

Figure 6.4   A Two-Dimensional Linear Model With Unstable Spirals

NOTE: The direction of movement is outward and away from the initial conditions (the dots) as indicated by the arrows.

of the eigenvalues. From Euler's formula, we can rewrite complex numbers in terms of sine and cosine, and we do this to obtain real-valued solutions to our linear differential equation with complex eigenvalues (Blanchard et al., 2006, pp. 293–296). While the imaginary parts of complex eigenvalues are responsible for the oscillatory overtime behavior of the dependent variables, the real parts are still responsible for whether the equilibrium will be a sink, a source, or a center. If the real part of the complex eigenvalue is positive, the trajectories will spiral outward away from the origin, and the equilibrium point is a spiral source.

Figure 6.4 presents the phase diagram for our system with complex eigenvalues with positive real parts. Four initial conditions are shown. Note that all trajectories spiral outward and away from the origin. With these parameter values, the origin is an unstable equilibrium point.

Stable Spirals

We now use parameter values $a = -1, b = 4, c = -2$, and $k = -1$. If the real part of the complex eigenvalue is negative, then the trajectories in phase

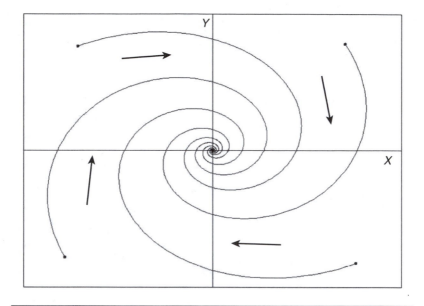

Figure 6.5   A Two-Dimensional Linear Model With Stable Spirals

NOTE: The direction of movement is inward and away from the initial conditions (the dots) as indicated by the arrows.

space spiral inward toward the origin, and the equilibrium point is a sink. The eigenvalues for this system are now $\lambda_i = -1 \pm i\sqrt{8}$. The negative real parts to the solutions produce a sink in the form of a stable spiral. A phase diagram of this system is presented in Figure 6.5. There are four initial conditions represented in this figure. Note that all four trajectories spiral inward toward the origin, which in this case is a stable equilibrium point.

Ellipses

Our final category of equilibria for first-order linear differential equation systems is an ellipse. Ellipses form as a result of having purely imaginary eigenvalues. That is, the real components of the eigenvalues are zero. If we assign parameter values for our system as $a = 1$, $b = 4$, $c = -2$, and $k = -1$, then the eigenvalues are $\lambda_i = \pm i\sqrt{7}$. A phase diagram of this system is presented in Figure 6.6. Now the origin is called a "center," and all trajectories forever orbit this center. A center is stable, and it is the only type of stable equilibrium point that is not asymptotic.

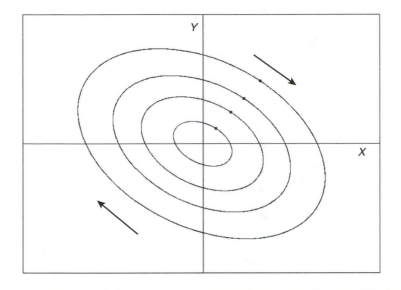

Figure 6.6   A Two-Dimensional Linear Model With Ellipses and a Center

NOTE: The directions of movement are shown by the arrows.

Summarizing the Stability Criteria

The stability criteria for linear differential equation systems of any dimension can be neatly summarized using a graphical portrayal of the complex plane, as is shown in Figure 6.7. In Figure 6.7, the x-axis represents the real parts of a system's eigenvalues, whereas the y-axis represents the imaginary parts. The current discussion is similar to that of May's (1974, pp. 23–26) with respect to the application of such techniques to model ecosystems. This helps address the issue of completeness with respect to analytical solutions for all categories of linear differential equation systems, although in a highly compact manner suitable for this book. Readers desiring a more detailed discussion can find it in any number of longer texts on differential equations. (See, e.g., Blanchard et al., 2006.)

The issue is how to represent the qualitative behavior of linear differential equations in such a way as to tie together the essential ingredients of their behavior with their associated eigenvalues. From Equation 6.21 we can see that a system of linear differential equations will grow explosively (due to the exponential factor) as time continues if any of the eigenvalues have positive real parts. All such systems must be considered unstable in

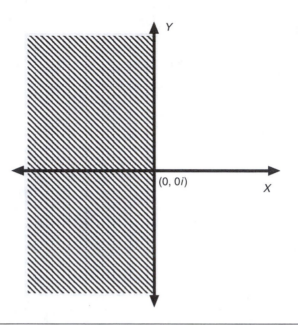

(0, 0i)

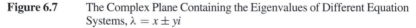

Figure 6.7   The Complex Plane Containing the Eigenvalues of Different Equation
Systems, $\lambda = x \pm yi$

NOTE: Stable systems require negative real parts, which is the hatched region of the complex plane.

the sense that they lack convergent properties with respect to the equilibrium. If all the eigenvalues have negative real parts, then the system will converge over time and remain stable. Moreover, the system will exhibit oscillatory behavior if any of the eigenvalues have imaginary components. Thus, systems with imaginary components and all negative real parts will have trajectories that spiral into the equilibrium. Such systems are oscillatory but stable. Systems with imaginary components and at least one positive real part will spiral outward away from the equilibrium. These are unstable oscillatory systems. Neutral stability is achieved with a steady orbit around an equilibrium, and that occurs in situations in which at least one of the eigenvalues is purely imaginary, so long as the real parts of the remaining eigenvalues are negative. From this discussion we can see that the trajectories in the neighborhood of an equilibrium for a linear system of differential equations will achieve stability if all their eigenvalues reside in the left-hand (hatched) side of Figure 6.7. Readers should note that we will find use for Figure 6.7 again in the next chapter when we discuss the stability criteria in the neighborhood of an equilibrium for a nonlinear system.

7. STABILITY ANALYSES OF NONLINEAR DIFFERENTIAL EQUATION SYSTEMS

The discussion in the previous chapter regarding the stability of systems of linear first-order differential equations near an equilibrium point can be extended to the nonlinear case. This is exceptionally important, since a great many social scientific models are nonlinear. Indeed, the linear models are more the exception than the rule.

The problem of evaluating systems of nonlinear differential equations is that the coefficient matrix **A** found in Equation 6.12 does not exist in the nonlinear case. However, this problem is readily solved by realizing that one can linearize nonlinear models for areas in phase space that reside within the neighborhood of an equilibrium. That is, when we are examining the stability of a nonlinear system in the proximity of an equilibrium point, we can use a linear form of the nonlinear system to obtain an accurate portrayal of the nonlinear system's behavior in that area. In general, nonlinear systems behave the same as linear systems in close proximity to equilibrium points. While it is possible to devise an exception to this, such exceptions are rarely encountered in practice. This means that we can continue to rely on our six stability categories for equilibria that were developed in the previous chapter even though we are now working with nonlinear systems.

The Jacobian

The key to linearizing any system of nonlinear differential equations is to construct the Jacobian matrix (or simply, the "Jacobian") of the system. The Jacobian is the linearized equivalent of the coefficient matrix **A** in Equation 6.12. While most disciplines call this matrix the Jacobian, some disciplines use other terminology. For example, in studies of population biology, the Jacobian is often called the "community matrix" (see, e.g., the classic work by May, 1974). The Jacobian is created by first taking the partial derivatives of each equation with respect to all of the dependent variables, and then substituting the equilibrium values of the dependent variables into those expressions. The first row of the Jacobian corresponds with the first equation of the system, the second row of the Jacobian corresponds with the second equation of the system, and so on. The first column of the Jacobian corresponds with the first dependent variable, the second column of the Jacobian corresponds with the second dependent variable, and so on. All of this exactly parallels the structure of coefficient matrix **A** in Equation 6.12 with respect to linear systems. (Indeed, the Jacobian of a linear system *is* the coefficient matrix **A**.)

For example, in a situation of a system of two differential equations with two dependent variables $[f(x, y), g(x, y)]$, the Jacobian would be

$$\mathbf{J} = \begin{pmatrix} \frac{\partial f(x^*, y^*)}{\partial x} & \frac{\partial f(x^*, y^*)}{\partial y} \\ \frac{\partial g(x^*, y^*)}{\partial x} & \frac{\partial g(x^*, y^*)}{\partial y} \end{pmatrix}. \tag{7.1}$$

Again, note that we must evaluate the Jacobian at the equilibrium point whose stability is being investigated.

After obtaining the Jacobian from a nonlinear system evaluated at a particular equilibrium point, stability analysis proceeds in the normal manner as with linear systems as described in the previous chapter. That is, one obtains the eigenvalues of the Jacobian just as they were obtained for the coefficient matrix $\mathbf{A}$ in Equation 6.12. Once the eigenvalues are obtained, one characterizes the behavioral quality of the nonlinear system *in the close neighborhood of the equilibrium point* in terms of the six categories of equilibria stability as discussed in the previous chapter with respect to linear systems (i.e., unstable nodes, stable nodes, saddles, unstable spirals, stable spirals, and centers). It is important to emphasize that this type of linearized stability analysis only works in close proximity to an equilibrium point. Beyond that, numerical and graphical methods of the type presented in previous chapters should be used. How close is close? This all depends on the relative influence of the nonlinear terms as one moves farther away from an equilibrium point. This should become clear in the discussion below.

At this point it is useful to step back and ask why a linearized version of a nonlinear system should work to evaluate the stability characteristics of an equilibrium point, and why this linearized version will normally not work farther away from the equilibrium. If we begin with our two nonlinear differential equations,

$$dx/dt = f(x, y),$$
$$dy/dt = g(x, y),$$

we can ask how this system behaves in the neighborhood of the equilibrium point (x_0, y_0). Let us move this equilibrium point to the origin with the change of variables

$$u = x - x_0, \tag{7.2}$$
$$z = y - y_0. \tag{7.3}$$

It is now obvious that the new variables will be near the origin when x and y are near the equilibrium point. (See also Blanchard et al., 2006, pp. 458–460.)

We can easily rewrite the system in terms of the new variables u and z. Since x_0 and y_0 are constants,

$$du/dt = d(x - x_0)/dt = dx/dt = f(x, y),$$
$$dz/dt = d(y - y_0)/dt = dy/dt = g(x, y).$$

From Equations 7.2 and 7.3, we can now say

$$du/dt = f(x_0 + u, y_0 + z),$$
$$dz/dt = g(x_0 + u, y_0 + z).$$

Near the origin, u and z approach zero, and at equilibrium

$$du/dt = f(x_0, y_0) = 0, \qquad\qquad\qquad [7.4]$$
$$dz/dt = g(x_0, y_0) = 0. \qquad\qquad\qquad [7.5]$$

Once we have moved the equilibrium point to the origin through the change of variables, we note that the nonlinear terms will be smaller in magnitude than the linear terms in the proximity of the equilibrium. For example, if $x = 0.1$ and $y = 0.1$, then $xy = 0.01$. Thus, the linear terms dominate the system near the equilibrium point. The best linear approximation for any two interdependent functions is the tangent plane, which is the same as the linear terms of the Taylor polynomial approximation for the functions. Thus we have,

$$\frac{du}{dt} \approx f(x_0, y_0) + \left[\frac{\partial f}{\partial x}(x_0, y_0)\right] u + \left[\frac{\partial f}{\partial y}(x_0, y_0)\right] z, \qquad [7.6]$$

$$\frac{dz}{dt} \approx g(x_0, y_0) + \left[\frac{\partial g}{\partial x}(x_0, y_0)\right] u + \left[\frac{\partial g}{\partial y}(x_0, y_0)\right] z. \qquad [7.7]$$

Note that the first term on the right-hand side of both Equations 7.6 and 7.7 vanishes due to Equations 7.4 and 7.5. If you write what remains of Equations 7.6 and 7.7 in matrix notation, you have

$$\begin{pmatrix} du/dt \\ dz/dt \end{pmatrix} \approx \mathbf{J} \begin{pmatrix} u \\ z \end{pmatrix},$$

where $\mathbf{J}$ is the Jacobian as defined in Equation 7.1.

Note that the change of variables to u and z was needed only to show that the nonlinear terms vanish near the equilibrium. We no longer need the change in variables to evaluate the stability of the differential equation system. We only need the Jacobian, and the Jacobian depends only on the original variables x and y.

While the above discussion involving the change in variables and the Jacobian finds correspondence with both the notation and emphasis favored by Blanchard et al. (2006, pp. 458–460), readers should note that this is not the way this subject has traditionally been presented in the literature on differential equations. I favor the above approach since it is both intuitive and quite general. However, readers will note that the more common approach is to model perturbations around an equilibrium point to see if those perturbations decay or grow. If they decay, then the equilibrium is stable since trajectories fall back to the equilibrium value. If they grow, then the trajectories move away from the equilibrium value, and the equilibrium is thus unstable. Both approaches use the Jacobian. The main difference between this approach and the approach that I favor is that the change of variables is not used with the former. Rather, the Taylor series approximation is made around the equilibrium point directly. While this is mathematically identical to that which I have presented above, what is lost is an intuitive understanding of why the nonlinear terms are of lower magnitude around the equilibrium and can thus be discarded. When one thinks of the equilibrium as being shifted to the origin, this realization is obvious. A useful discussion of the more traditional method of presenting this subject from the perspective of population biology can be found in the classic treatment by May (1974, pp. 19–26). For a social science application, see also Huckfeldt et al. (1982, pp. 40–42).

An Example

Let us reconsider the nonlinear predator-prey model (Equations 3.1 and 3.2) from the perspective of this chapter. Let us use the parameter values that were used to create Figure 3.3. These parameter values are $a = 1$, $b = 1, c = 3, e = 1, m = 0$, and $n = 0$. We have already seen using a phase diagram that these parameter values produce elliptical orbits around the system's center, the equilibrium point (1/3, 1). We want to confirm this using an analysis of the system's Jacobian. The system is now as shown in Equations 7.8 and 7.9.

$$dX/dt = X - XY, \qquad [7.8]$$
$$dY/dt = 3XY - Y. \qquad [7.9]$$

The Jacobian for this system is

$$\mathbf{J} = \begin{pmatrix} 1 - y^* & -x^* \\ 3y^* & 3x^* - 1 \end{pmatrix} = \begin{pmatrix} 0 & -1/3 \\ 3 & 0 \end{pmatrix},$$

where x^* and y^* are the equilibrium values 1/3 and 1, respectively.

Now we want the eigenvalues that arise from substituting the equilibrium values into the Jacobian and solving

$$\mathbf{det} \begin{pmatrix} 0 - \lambda & -1/3 \\ 3 & 0 - \lambda \end{pmatrix} = 0.$$

This produces the characteristic equation $\lambda^2 + 1 = 0$, or $\lambda = \pm\sqrt{-1}$. Thus, $\lambda = \pm i$, a purely imaginary result. From the results of the previous chapter with respect to linear systems, we know that solutions to this system form an ellipse with the center (1/3, 1). Our only restriction in using the methods of this chapter is the knowledge that our conclusion regarding the elliptical behavior of the dependent variables applies only to the area in phase space that is located in the local neighborhood of the equilibrium. It may sometimes occur that the trajectory behaviors persist further away from the equilibrium, as is the case with this example. But this is the exception more than the rule with respect to nonlinear models, and when it does occur, it needs to be confirmed using other methods, such as with an examination of direction field and flow diagrams.

Summary

This chapter extends our discussion of differential equations to the analysis of nonlinear systems. Many interesting differential equation applications will have nonlinear components, so limiting our capabilities to the linear case is not really an option. With the nonlinear case, we are interested in characterizing the stability of any given system in the neighborhood of an equilibrium. Doing this is part of a more complete analysis of the system, one that would incorporate other methods as well—such as the graphical techniques presented in this book—to evaluate some of the more global characteristics of the system. Crucial to the stability analysis of nonlinear systems is the Jacobian. The Jacobian allows one to linearize the system in the neighborhood of an equilibrium, thereby enabling one to conduct standard stability tests based on the system's eigenvalues. We can now return to Figure 6.7 and find that it is equally appropriate for characterizing the stability of a system as with the linear case. The differences are that with the nonlinear case one is locating the eigenvalues of the localized Jacobian in Figure 6.7 rather than the eigenvalues of an entire linear system and that the stability characterization is limited in the nonlinear case to the neighborhood of the equilibrium.

8. FRONTIERS OF EXPLORATION

Cyclical behaviors of all types (chaotic or otherwise) are hugely relevant to human behavior. We sleep each night and wake up each morning. We eat food at periodic intervals. We conduct our elections in regular cycles of defined length. We collect census data at regular intervals, normally each decade. We conduct population surveys according to our other electoral and social cycles. Our behaviors even follow the seasons; we swim each summer and ski each winter. In general, humans nearly always repeat themselves. Both differential and difference equations are ideal for analyzing periodic behaviors of many types, and social scientists have often exploited such equations to great benefit. The study of our vast array of human cycles is one example of a great frontier relevant to the application of differential equations. It is not an entirely unexplored frontier by any means. It is just that there remains much that we do not yet know about ourselves and our cycles. It is also one reason why this is an exciting time among those of us who seek to apply differential equation modeling in our scientific research.

This book represents a beginning in the study of differential equations. There are many areas within the study of differential equations that have not been covered here. For example, it is possible to create dynamical systems that cannot be easily analyzed using only the graphical methods suggested in previous chapters, such as phase diagrams, direction field diagrams, vector field diagrams, and so on. It is not that such methods are useless but that supplemental tools are needed to address some of the problems encountered in more complex settings. This can happen when cyclical behavior does not readily repeat itself, a characteristic of chaotic differential equation systems with three or more dimensions (see Brown, 1995b). This also happens with many nonautonomous systems of two dimensions, when the independent variable t is explicitly included within the equations. In nonautonomous situations, the vector field (defined by the differential equations themselves) changes as time moves forward. Additional methods (such as Poincaré maps) that go beyond the scope of this book will be called into play in the analysis of such systems.

In general, many interesting differential equation systems can be made to produce chaotic results, and indeed, chaos is quite the norm in nature. For example, when water molecules flow down a river, it is impossible to predict their ultimate precise location downstream based on knowledge of their location upstream regardless of our knowledge of the laws of physics that govern their movement. It is not that we simply do not have enough information. Rather, it is a characteristic of such systems that a seemingly insignificant change in the initial conditions can produce large differences in behavior over time. Again, I have written about this elsewhere (Brown, 1995b), and this is a good next step for those students who wish to pursue the subject of differential equations further.

In many areas of mathematics, an undergraduate college student really has little hope of encountering math at a level on which scholars are doing active research. One needs to be fairly far along in graduate study in math in order to see what the "big guns" are doing in real time. But the study of differential equations is different. It is one area in which undergraduate students can confront the same problems that advanced researchers are encountering. This is one of the reasons why the study of differential equations is so exciting today. You do not have to go very far into the subject before you are on at least one of the frontiers of research.

If this is true of the study of differential equations in general, it becomes obvious that this is even more true with respect to the application of differential equations in the social sciences. While there are numerous examples in the extant literature of exemplary applications of differential equations that address important social scientific problems (a variety of which I have mentioned in this book), it is just as true that we have so far seen only the tip of the iceberg in terms of what is possible. For social scientists, the frontier is much larger than the fully explored territory. For those students of this subject who seek excitement, know that you are in the right place at the right time, however linear or nonlinear your perceptions of the future may be.

REFERENCES

Aczel, A. D. (2003). *Entanglement: The unlikely story of how scientists, mathematicians, and philosophers proved Einstein's spookiest theory.* New York: Plume.

Atkinson, K. (1985). *Elementary numerical analysis.* New York: Wiley.

Berelson, B. R., Lazarsfeld, P. F., & McPhee, W. N. (1954). *Voting: A study of opinion formation in a presidential campaign.* Chicago: University of Chicago Press.

Blanchard, P., Devaney, R. L., & Hall, G. R. (2006). *Differential equations* (3rd ed.). Belmont, CA: Thomson—Brooks/Cole.

Boyce, W. E., & DiPrima, R. C. (1977). *Elementary differential equations and boundary value problems* (3rd ed.). New York: Wiley.

Braun, M. (1983). *Differential equations and their applications.* New York: Springer-Verlag.

Brown, C. (with MacKuen, M.). (1987a). On political context and attitude change. *American Political Science Review, 81*(2), 471–490.

Brown, C. (1987b). Mobilization and party competition within a volatile electorate. *American Sociological Review, 52*(1), 59–72.

Brown, C. (1988). Mass dynamics of U.S. presidential competitions, 1928–36. *American Political Science Review, 82*(4), 1153–1181.

Brown, C. (1991). *Ballots of tumult: A portrait of volatility in American voting.* Ann Arbor: University of Michigan Press.

Brown, C. (1993). Nonlinear transformation in a landslide: Johnson and Goldwater in 1964. *American Journal of Political Science, 37*(2), 582–609.

Brown, C. (1994). Politics and the environment: Nonlinear instabilities dominate. *American Political Science Review, 88*(2), 292–303.

Brown, C. (1995a). *Serpents in the sand: Essays on the nonlinear nature of politics and human destiny.* Ann Arbor: University of Michigan Press.

Brown, C. (1995b). *Chaos and catastrophe theories.* Series: Quantitative Applications in the Social Sciences, Number 107. Thousand Oaks, CA: Sage.

Brown, C. (2008). *Graph algebra: Mathematical modeling with a systems approach.* Series: Quantitative Applications in the Social Sciences. Thousand Oaks, CA: Sage.

Campbell, A., Converse, P. E., Miller, W., & Stokes, D. E. (1960). *The American voter.* New York: Wiley.

Coleman, J. S. (1964). *Introduction to mathematical sociology.* New York: Free Press.

Coleman, J. S., Katz, E., & Menzel, H. (1957). The diffusion of an innovation among physicians. *Sociometry, 20,* 253–270.

Cortés, F., Przeworski, A., & Sprague, J. (1974). *Systems analysis for social scientists.* New York: Wiley.

Crosby, R. W. (1987). Toward a classification of complex systems. *European Journal of Operational Research 30,* 291–293.

Danby, J. M. A. (1997). *Computer modeling: From sports to spaceflight ... from order to chaos.* Richmond, VA: Willmann-Bell.

Engel, J. H. (1954). A verification of Lanchester's law. *Operations Research, 2,* 163–171.

Forrester, J. W. (1971). *World dynamics.* Cambridge, MA: Wright-Allen Press.

Gottman, J. M., Murray, J. D., Swanson, C., Tyson, R., & Swanson, K. R. (2003). *The mathematics of marriage: Dynamic nonlinear models.* Cambridge: MIT Press.

Hadley, G. (1961). *Linear algebra.* Reading, MA: Addison-Wesley.

Hamming, R. W. (1971). *Introduction to applied numerical analysis.* New York: McGraw-Hill.

Hamming, R. W. (1973). *Numerical methods for scientists and engineers* (2nd ed.). New York: McGraw-Hill.

Hirsch, M. W., & Smale, S. (1974). *Differential equations, dynamical systems, and linear algebra.* New York: Academic Press.

Huckfeldt, R. R., Kohfeld, C. W., & Likens, T. W. (1982). *Dynamic modeling: An introduction.* Newbury Park, CA: Sage.

Kadera, K. (2001). *The power-conflict story: A dynamic model of interstate rivalry.* Ann Arbor: University of Michigan Press.

Koçak, H. (1989). *Differential and difference equations through computer experiments with a supplementary diskette containing PHASER: An animator/simulator for dynamical systems for IBM personal computers* (2nd ed.). New York: Springer-Verlag.

Lanchester, F. W. (1916). *Aircraft in warfare: The dawn of the fourth arm.* London: Tiptree, Constable and Company.

Lotka, A. J. (1925). *Elements of physical biology.* Baltimore: Williams and Wilkins.

Malthus, T. (1999). *An essay on the principle of population.* Oxford: Oxford University Press. (Original work published 1798)

May, R. M. (1974). *Stability and complexity in model ecosystems* (2nd ed.). Princeton, NJ: Princeton University Press.

Mesterton-Gibbons, M. (1989). *A concrete approach to mathematical modeling.* New York: Addison-Wesley.

Morris, M., & Brown, O. E. (1952). *Differential equations* (3rd ed.). New York: Prentice-Hall.

Przeworski, A. (1975). Institutionalization of voting patterns, or is mobilization the source of decay. *American Political Science Review, 69*(1), 49–67.

Przeworski, A., & Soares, G. A. D. (1971). Theories in search of a curve: A contextual interpretation of left vote. *American Political Science Review, 65* (1), 51–68.

Przeworski, A., & Sprague, J. (1986). *Paper stones: A history of electoral socialism.* Chicago: University of Chicago Press.

Rapoport, A. (1960). *Fights, games and debates.* Ann Arbor: University of Michigan Press.

Rapoport, A. (1983). *Mathematical models in the social and behavioral sciences.* New York: Wiley.

Richardson, L. F. (1960). *Arms and insecurity.* Chicago: Quadrangle Books.

Simon, H. A. (1957). *Models of man: Social and rational.* New York: Wiley.

Tuma, N. B., & Hannan, M. T. (1984). *Social dynamics: Models and methods.* New York: Academic Press.

Volterra, V. (1930). *Theory of functionals.* L. Fantappiè (Ed.). (M. Long, Trans.) Glasgow: Blackie.

Volterra, V. (1931). *Theorie mathématique de la lutte pour la vie.* Paris: Gauthier-Villars.

Zill, D. G. (2005). *A first course in differential equations with modeling applications.* Belmont, CA: Thomson—Brooks/Cole.

INDEX

ABOUT THE AUTHOR

Courtney Brown began his teaching career as a college calculus instructor in Africa before moving on to teach nonlinear differential and difference equation modeling in the social sciences at the University of California at Los Angeles, Emory University, and the Interuniversity Consortium for Political and Social Research Summer Program at the University of Michigan. He has published numerous books on applied nonlinear mathematical modeling in the social sciences, including *Serpents in the Sand: Essays on the Nonlinear Nature of Politics and Human Destiny, Ballots of Tumult: A Portrait of Volatility in American Voting, Chaos and Catastrophe Theories,* and *Graph Algebra: Mathematical Modeling With a Systems Approach.* Also of scholarly interest, although independent of his mathematical and social science work as a college professor, he has published a science book on the subject of nonlocal consciousness and physics, *Remote Viewing: The Science and Theory of Nonphysical Perception,* an area of research that has gained attention in select physics and psychology circles. He received his PhD degree from Washington University, St. Louis in 1981 in political science with an emphasis on mathematical modeling.